RHYMES
AND
REASONS

FOR
ALL
SEASONS

By Kathleen Pell Rizzo

INTRODUCTION

Welcome to "Rhymes and Reasons for All Seasons," a collection of poems that reflect my personality and help me come to terms with heartaches, conflicts and lessons, as well as all the joys of love and life and nature.

Therapy and healing come in many different forms and for me, rhyming has always helped me process the ups and downs of life's journey.

Even if you have never been a fan of poetry, I think you will find my writings very 'down to earth,' relatable, and even amusing.

I hope my poetry will touch your heart and tickle your funny bone too!

In addition to poetry, I've written and illustrated collections of humorous stories, including a play. I'm always happy to share my writing at fundraising events, libraries, clubs, organizations, and private parties.

Finally, I want to say thank you from the bottom of my heart to all the friends, family and colleagues who have supported my writing over the years (you know who you are!) including those who helped me assemble this book. Thank you and much love!

Kathie Pell Rizzo

Table of Contents

iv

1. SPRING

Seasons of Life

The message of the seasons is profound
For things we cannot see are soon to be
Like changes taking place beneath the ground
The awesomeness of life in mystery.

The vividness of Summer and of Fall
The sun infatuation we enjoyed
Desire for perfection in us all
The darkness we keep choosing to avoid.

Yet Truth is constant as the Evergreen
Thriving in the shadows and the sun
Enduring all conditions unforeseen
Through the changing seasons – every one.

The Winter snow, a heavy insulation
All the earth in muffled stillness waits
An inner voice that urges to be patient
While nature in her wisdom contemplates.

The ice upon the lake in solid form
Underlying secrets of the soul
Where life sustained below remains the norm
The place where self-discoveries unfold.

Some species are renewed by shedding skin
Others just awaken from their sleep
It's best to seek our changes from within
The stirrings down beneath the frozen deep.

Winter – Spring, a contrast in complexion
Flowers reappear in all their glory
From snowy white – a colorful selection
Seasons of life repeat the ageless story.

Spring returns regardless of the weather
Hopes and dreams revealed in daffodils
Birds and creatures nesting as they gather
Instinctively their destiny fulfills.

Reality presents in every hue
Buds and blossoms attracting our focus
Subconsciously from them we take our cue
Display our truths as boldly as the crocus.

Starting over – transforming like the earth
The spirit with the natural law in sync
Embraces once again the path of birth
Re-Creation from The Source to which we link.

The seasons exit and in their aftermath
The lessons of the earth are all around
Revelations sprout along the path
By Summer – fruitful clarity abounds.

We stand among the Evergreens and Oaks
Survive the frigid cold and stormy weather
We sway and bend under the windy strokes
Family – and forest holding fast together.

03–22–10

Surprise

At Winter's end — the end did bring
With hardly a chance to welcome Spring —
Little by little she took her leave
Her absence we still cannot believe.

We rejoice that the suffering — is through
But how will the seasons ever renew?
Yet Spring still blossomed in all its glory
And Summertime came and sang its story.

Hope is renewed in Autumn's colors
Like the unconditional love of mothers!
So Fall pays its visit once again
Warm and welcome as a faithful friend.

Bearing gifts of Burgundy and Gold —
As Nature's annual mysteries unfold.
Those of us who gratefully remain —
Are filled with awesomeness we can't contain!

Vibrant colors delight our eyes!
As the changing seasons take us by surprise!
And once again our hearts are singing —
In chorus with joyful spirits ringing!

When cold of Winter returns our way
We'll count our blessings every day
And laugh with memories still alive
Love — much like the seasons will survive!

10–19–13

4

Awakening!

Suddenly there are Daffodils!
And Crocuses appear!!
Colors heralding the onset –
Nature's favorite time of year!

Doves are nesting near my window!
Busy Robins on the lawn!!
Bunnies posing next to Tulips –
In the woods – a wobbly Fawn!

Rainy downfalls soak the garden!
Bicycles return to play!!
I can't see my neighbor's yard now –
Forsythias are in the way!

Chirping chorus in the treetops!
Not a trace of last week's snow!!
Buds are bursting on the branches –
Ants are marching down below!

Seems I went to bed in Winter!
And awoke to early Spring!!
Yesterdays have finally melted –
Now my healing heart takes wing!

Time to open up the windows!
Take a walk in just a sweater!!
Green is such a pleasant outlook –
All is well or getting better!

04–01–06

Signs of Spring – and Everything!!

Forsythias are yellow –
Daffodils are too
Spring has arrived
And Winter is through!

Kindergarten friends
Are spying around
On big sentence charts
They told what they've found.

There are buds on the trees –
And nests filled with birds
On the Kindergarten Word Wall
There are 44 words!!

They wrote them all down
So they will not forget
Are they proud of themselves
That they're reading? You bet!!

Inspired by reading
They made booklets and kites
There's no end to adventure
Once the reading bug bites!

They cooked Green Eggs and Ham
And enjoyed it for sure
There's a picture as proof
Hanging up on the door!

Writing sentences now
Is an everyday thing
They write about weekends
And flowers in Spring!

What has tulips and bumble bees
And looks like a garden?
No it's not the park
You're in Kindergarten!!

Mrs. Rizzo 04–14–05

Beautiful, Bountiful Spring

Golden yellow daffodils
and tulips all in rows
A chorus line of colors
fills the garden as it grows.

Early risers – crocuses –
then bright forsythias
(Sad for anyone who misses
their delightful stay with us!

Be careful not to lose a day –
even in the rain
For quickly they will pass away –
'til Spring returns again.)

Branches newly rustling –
and dressed in emerald green
I'm wide eyed at the fullness –
as if I've never seen!

Spring is meant to dazzle –
experience rebirth by surprise
Renew and refresh and restore the soul –
and open up our eyes!

Hyacinths in soft pastels –
Rhododendrons – grand and showy!
(That bush's name I could not tell –
way back when it was snowy!)

Gentle geraniums and delicate dogwood –
in visual harmony
A stroke from the brush of He Who sees Good –
and paints it artistically!

Vivid Azaleas and hearty Hydrangeas –
an eye feast fit for a King!
Impatience spreading as if they're contagious –
Beautiful, Bountiful Spring!!

The blushing Lily of the Valley
hides and vibrates in the breeze
A gathering of tiny brides –
underneath the trees.

Careful stepping as you go –
while treading in the garden
Pretty pansies laying low –
seem to beg our pardon.

Watch them smiling and wiggling –
while waving hello and good-bye
Hear them girlishly giggling –
for Pansies are lovely – but shy.

Sweet Cherry Blossoms and luscious Magnolias –
burst on the stage all in pink!
Gracefully posed and wearing that color –
inspired the Ballet I think!!

Irises – frivolous and frilly –
flapping their colorful tongues!
Bob in the breeze willy-nilly –
bold purple, mustard and white ones!

Then comes the Roses in glorious blooms –
of yellow, red, pink, white and peach!
Filling our nostrils with heavenly perfumes –
as far as our noses will reach!!

I'm glad when I see the Roses –
for the promise of Summer they bring
And – I'm grateful to God to have witnessed again –
Beautiful, Bountiful Spring!

05–21–09

Mother Nature's Gift – "Pretty in Pink"

It snowed Pink on Mother's Day –
with blossoms all around!
Pink doilies underneath the trees –
Pink frillies on the ground!

The wild breezes blew and sent –
Pink flurries through the air –
A pretty Pink phenomenon –
that made us smile and stare!

With every gust the trees released –
a burst of Pink confetti!
From morning until evening –
like a blizzard Pink and steady!

Softly spinning petals –
pirouetting in the breeze –
Spring turned into Wonderland –
Pink snow without the freeze!!

It's May! The temperature is warm!
The sky is blue and sunny!
Mother Nature's gift on Mother's Day –
now doesn't that sound funny?!

Though Mother's Day is over –
still the yard is frosted Pink!
This was a Special Mother's Day –
the Loveliest I think!!!

May 2015

Diana's Daffodils

Diana's daffodils sprung up
Hearty green and new!
Yellow golden trumpeteers
Herald nature's cue!

The snow has barely melted
Scattered patches still remain
The temperature denies it
But Spring has come again!

The season came on quickly
Shook me from my solitude
Yellow blooms have opened
Unfolding changes in my mood.

I prefer to stay in Winter
With Diana by my side
But Daffodils are leading
With Diana as my guide!

A message from Diana
Coded yellow in the yard
'The seasons that will follow –
Just might not be so hard.'

She brightened up my life
She promised she would stay
I'm grateful she delivered
Daffodils to light my way!

04–01–07

Observing Spring

Winter melts and nothing's left
but dampness all around
'Til tufts of grass and crocuses
break through the softened ground.

A month ago the roadside was
a stark and snowy slope
Now little green appearances
of joy and love and hope!

A scattering of Violets
beside a rocky knoll
Strewn with fallen branches
depicting Winter's toll.

Red and orange, pink and purple
Tulips by the dozens
Buttery Forsythia
and Daffodils their cousins

Pastels on the hillside
in impressionistic style
Robins on the front lawn –
It's enough to make you smile!

A bunny in the backyard
hopping 'round and nibbling
Kathie still and pensive,
stirring up a poem for scribbling!

The lake returns from Iceland
and reflects the sun with luster
A brand new brood of ducklings
follows mama in a cluster!

A bumblebee darts here and there,
his first day on the job
Two hawks inspect a treetop
for a blackbird's nest to rob.

Nature's sequence of events –
a cycle never weary
Observe the little details
of the woods' itinerary.

Every day another sign
of life and hope and love
Awakened in the senses
by the cooing of a dove.

Officially it's Springtime! –
Nature issues her decree
A woodpecker is tapping
out the message on a tree!

The changing of the seasons –
Don't ever take for granted
Tune in to the chorus
of the song of Spring recanted!

My spirit is brought to its knees
as I'm drawn to the sight of each flower
The whispering newness of the trees –
all speak of a Higher Power.

The rainbows that we cannot touch –
are certainly still there
Spring remains the valid proof –
that God is everywhere.

Just listen to the treetops
and the sound of chirping birds
A melody He sends to us –
a love song without words.

And think about the blowing wind –
we feel but cannot see
Deny the wind? Deny His Grace –
displayed so openly??

Spring is meant to touch the soul
and open up the senses
Restore – renew and make us whole
and overcome pretenses.

Back to beauty – back to life
back to knowing Love
Back to understanding
God is here – not just up above.

04-05-10

15

Is That a Crocus I See??

The crocuses always surprise me
I never expect their arrival!
It's hard to believe –
On a cold Winter's eve –
Underground they maintain their survival.

Just when the Winter seems endless
And impatience is starting to show
I am caught by surprise –
Right before my own eyes –
The Crocuses started to grow!!

I live for the onset of Spring
The tender and promise of green
The shooting and sprouting –
After cold Winter doubting –
Look! Robins are back on the scene!!

The Crocuses always amaze me
A subtle, effective endurance
That awakens the Season
And gives me good reason
To celebrate Spring's reassurance!

Before the last snowfall of Winter
They bravely protrude through the earth
And faithfully appear
Every year after year –
A prelude to glorious rebirth!!

Bridal the white little heads
And Royal the purple and gold
When Mother Nature says "NOW!"
Old Man Winter must bow –
To the Crocuses brazen and bold!!

03–22–09

First Day of Spring – 2018

I made it through winter without you –
I wouldn't have thought that I could.

Managed Buick and basement and boiler –
and paid all the bills that I should.

I put out the trash on Sundays and Wednesdays –
on Tuesdays recycled the rest –

I can even make pretty good coffee –
though you always made it the best.

When the snows came I cleaned off the car –
wishing that you were still here –

But I'm secure by your love-light at night –
and sleep soundly without any fear.

Still I stare at your picture again and again –
and long for the days that are gone –

Gone from my world – but forever in my heart –
our love will live on and on.

When winter is finally over –
the springtime will blossom anew –

And one day at a time I'll March 4th –
with a love-light inspired by you!

God willing the summer will follow –
by then the days will grow longer –

With sunshine and swimming and fresh air –
my heart will be stronger and stronger!

In time for the changes in autumn –
my heart too will then coincide –

All vibrant and bursting with colors –
when the leaves and my tears have all dried.

So that winter without you next year –
will not seem as harsh as before –

With family and friendships beside me –
and a brand new granddaughter in store!!

2. FAMILY

Newlyweds

I love him in the morning
When he sneaks away in silence
So careful not to move me
For the thought that I'll awaken.

Sometimes he whispers "Love ya Kath"
Before the sunlight enters
And he holds me and he kisses
And it's just the way I dreamed it in my dreams.

I love him in the evening
When I hear that welcome door slam
And his cheeks are red from football
And he's hungry and he kisses me.

He laughs and tells me all about
The things that make him famous
And I start to jump inside me
For his very voice excites me.

I love him in the night time
When he lets me rest upon him
And his breathing fascinates me
And I want to stay awake all night
Just to feel his love beside me.

And I love the way he touches
When I stir within my dreaming
I am certain now of heaven
And I pray for all eternity beside him.

1969

Man of My Dreams

The man of my dreams gets up way before me
To warm up the car and make coffee and tea.

He carries my bags and lays out my coat
(Sometimes in my lunch-bag he puts a love note!)

The man of my dreams cleans up after we eat
And later on the couch he massages my feet!

He serves Chamomile and draws me a bath
(And once in a while he says, 'Love-ya Kath'.)

The man of my dreams does the laundry – buys food
(Plays our favorite love songs to put me in the mood!)

Makes trips to the Post Office, the deli and bank
6 A.M. at the gas station to fill up my tank!

The man of my dreams is still handsome and strong
And still holds my hand — as if we were young.

Of his humor and good looks — I never will tire
(After 38 years — he can still light my fire!!)

As a friend and a neighbor — you couldn't ask more
As a son or a brother — and the Father of four!!!!

The man of my dreams is the Love of My Life
He's my friend and my Husband — and I'm his Dear
Wife!!!!!

01–13–08

23

Morning Complaints

It's cold, my love, when I arise
And rub the sleepies from my eyes
And hop across linoleum bare
To see your picture smiling there.

No refuge for a warm embrace
Just that playful Paulie smile
That teases in my search for shoes
As I stand shivering all the while!

The water greets me with a chill
Upon my dresser smiling still
You watch me light my cigarette
And say "You'll never quit, I bet!"

How can I even brush my hair
With you eternally grinning there?
The clock reveals my morning fate
"Hurry Kath, or you'll be late!"

How wicked to be smiling, Paul
While I am rushing through it all!
I wish my cold floor had a rug –
And my cold self – a morning hug!!

1967

The Ritual

"Good night-
I love you
   I love you"
And away
       away
         away.
The shadows of night left to shroud me
Alone
But he leaves me his words.
Words
"Good night-
I love you
   I love you"
Then away
       away
         away.
I go in –
But I do not live here.
I am empty
Existing in time.
Invading tomorrows
And dwelling
On words
     words
      words.
They hang from the clock
And my mind.
And play
     play
      play –
Molest me
Then sing me to sleep.

"Good night-
I love you
    I love you"
It hovers
The ghost of the day
It lingers
    and haunts
        and harasses
'Til the fingers of sleep bless my eyes.

Kathie Pell 1967

Last Night

Beautiful gifts he gives me
Sent on the wings of his words
That hover – then circle around my head
Then soar to the ends of my heart.
"One in heart" – 'Til I'm dizzy with joy!

And his heart is my vineyard
In his lips are contained the sweet wine
His mind can produce and deliver
And his lips can compose – as they sing
Intoxicating my mind
'Til I'm grinning and drunk with his poetry!

"One in mind" – He wraps it all neatly in silence
The forbidden fruit he conceals
Then waits for some fine golden moment
At the end of a fine golden day
Then quietly, gently commits them revealing
Some strange and sacred fruit!

In sinless celebration
We indulge and we share in the feast
"One in affections" – capacity holds no degree
For hunger and thirst unfulfilled
The promise must vow saturation
Not just food – but a share in the harvest
Not just wine – but a place in the vineyard
And in timeless anticipation
            I wait for
                A part in
                    His life.
                                Kathie Pell 1967

To Paul (Forever and Always)

Warm and velvety
New and sincere
Away whispered moments
To my heart through my ear
"Forever and always"
Our eyes meet and then
Away silent moments
'Til he whispers again
"Forever and always"
And the glow from his eyes
Reflects from his heart
I believe him and sigh
And I want to be part of this man
'Til I die
'Til – "Forever and always."

Kathie Pell 1968

Today

"Kathie the summer is leaving us"
    "Yes I know"
      I believed – and it left – just like that
      With his words
       And I wanted to cry but I couldn't.

      "Will you build us a house in Hohokus?"
"Yes – and in Adlers we'll sit by the fire"
      - In silence, in love with our dream.

"Someday...
I get up every morning Kath
 And I have no job to go to"
      "Yes I know – but you'll be great – someday."

"Hm," he said as he always does
      When things to be said can't be spoken.
      And that evening he sang for I asked him
      But his heart didn't harmonize
      And his eyes remained where they had been
      Glaring and heavy – and weary
      With the troubled self he was seeing
      And the words of his song corresponded
      And I wanted to cry but I couldn't.

"Good night love
Good sleep love
I'll call you tomorrow"
      Sleep can relieve him – not I.
      Then I sat down to read the newspaper
      For I knew that my bed would be cold.
      And his song remained with me all night –

"There's a place for us –
     U.S. GUNS KILL 72 OF ALLIES
"Somewhere a place for us –
     THREAT OF POLICE REVOLT EBBS
"Peace and quiet and open air –
     ANOTHER BOMB EXPLOSION...
"Waits for us somewhere –"

     So – I went to bed.

                Kathie Pell 1968

Work Work Work (to Paul)

Don't take me dancing
With the moon up above
Don't take me dancing
Don't slow down for love.

Don't let the music
Draw you too close to me
It might lead to romance
That once used to be.

Keep your mind on work dear
The fast lane's for you
But I'll take slow dancing
To my dreams I'll be true.

With your arms wrapped around me
We've got nothing to prove
With the music and the moment
We're in love as we move.

No – Don't take me dancing
Just can't take the time
Got to keep those wheels turnin'
While you're still in your prime.

I'll just keep on dreamin'
That I'm dancing with you
Hope the music's still playing
When your workin' is through.

Hopin' if you do take me
That the fire still burns
Like the dancers on the floor
Life is so filled with turns.

While you sit at your meeting
While you call your next play –
I'll be dreamin' of dancing
With my Lover (You!) someday.

My Daughter Marci

My daughter Marci has made me so proud
from the very first moment we met!

A good woman and daughter –
always doin' what she oughta –
livin' up to the ideals that she set.

She married a wonderful man! –
their love is a perfect fit!

As husband and wife they have made a good life –
and Mira just compliments it!!

They work very hard to get by –
give it their best, day by day –

The happy three – make a great family! –
sharing quality time – come what may!

Keeping in touch with Abuela and Nonna –
always looking out for our good!

When we need them – they're there –
always showing they care! –
with love and respect as they should

As parents to Mira they're awesome! –
that little girl is so blessed!!

Meet her every need – lots of stories they read! –
though at times they could sure use a rest!!

That Mira has stolen their hearts! –
her well-being always comes first!

With their home rearranged –
their lives forever changed –
to family life they are immersed!

I'm so proud! I can't say it enough!! –
they surely stepped up to the plate!!

With all they've achieved –
it just makes me believe –
joyful proof that it's never too late!!

I'm so happy that they live so near –
that I'm able to share in their lives –

To be useful is key and a blessing for me! –
with Mira, my purpose survives!

God bless this beautiful family! –
and I pray, keep them in your care –

Let cardinals keep showing –
to help them keep knowing –
Nonno's love is also still here!!!

My Son Marc

My son Marc – has always made me proud –
 a kind-hearted, generous man!

With musical talent, endowed –
making music was always his plan!

Dependable – there when he's needed! –
his family always comes first!

His love and devotion deep seeded! –
his caring makes a mother's heart burst!!

He opened his heart and his home –
providing his brother and wife –

A secure place for them – on loan –
in support of their family life.

He's crazy 'bout nephews and nieces –
and loves spending time when he can –

With jokes and tall stories – he teases! –
but always ready to lend us a hand.

Self-discipline is one of his traits –
his stamina must be admired!

To assist, he never hesitates –
keeps going long after he's tired!

In person or else on the phone –
he displays his care and concern –

Always calls me when I am alone –
says, "if you need me – you know I'll return."

That's the kind of man Marc is –
he's one in a million I think!

He's a caregiver and a musician –
ever ready to help in a blink!

I'm so happy he's found "Little C" –
she has certainly been such a blessing!

Is it serious? We'll just have to see –
But for now, he's not yet confessing

Like the others, he's always in my prayers –
in the night when I take up my beads –

He never fails to show how he cares –
for me and his whole family's needs.

And so I continue to pray –
for his happiness and well-being. Night and day –

And in thanksgiving for such a fine son! –
I'm so proud of the man he's become!!

My Dear Son Luke

My dear son Luke – the youngest of the brood –
now a loving husband and father –

A musical artist – and such a handsome dude! –
so in love with his girls and their mother!

My son Luke was the favorite baby brother –
he was such a welcome addition! –

The curly headed cutie – was spoiled like no other –
as the baby he attracted much attention!

We protected him and raised him with love –
with God's help to keep him on track –

Always praying for guidance from above –
of love and faith, there was never a lack.

He played sports and had lots of friends –
'til tragedy compromised his youth –

Life's roads has its twists and its bends –
and reality became a harsh truth!

The death of a friend is so cruel! –
every day it was hard to believe –

But Luke stayed focused and in school –
with a college degree to achieve.

And oh what a happy achievement! –
though forever he'll carry the scar –

Worked through his shock and bereavement –
time is still the best healer by far.

Attempting to teach – he was willing –
a few different places he tried –

But none of them turned out so thrilling –
his distaste for it he couldn't hide.

In the midst of employment confusion –
wasn't only the job was distasteful –

His love life had been an illusion –
he discovered his girlfriend unfaithful!

Oh the ups and downs of maturing! –
to such painful hurts we're subjected!!

Only by overcoming and enduring –
that from falling apart we're protected!

But Luke proved himself as a man –
by landing quite square on his feet! –

Continued the best that he can –
not knowing that true love he would meet!

My son Luke is a married man now –
with two little girls of his own!

The years have passed, though I don't know how –
through it all as a man he has grown!

Is it the love of his children and wife? –
is it the power of prayer? –

Is it the love he got early in life?
Does he realize how much we all care? –

May God continue to bless Luke, my son –
Andrea, Sofia and Camila! –

May heavenly grace surround everyone! –
from Poppy – and Tommy – and Teela!! :)

My Son Paul

My son Paul is strong and lean and tall –
and works hard to make a good life –

From morning 'til night – with all of his might –
for his wonderful children and wife!

At the crack of dawn – puts his best self on –
and makes all the rounds on the bus

He doesn't complain – in snow, sleet or rain –
shows up right on time as he must.

Shows his family he cares –
with the meals he prepares –
and serves them with ease and with pride!

At the table they gather –
kids, mother and father –
with talk, love and laughter on the side!

Their needs he can meet – with plenty to eat –
and a fireside cozy and warm –

He and his wife – have made a good life –
praying daily to keep them from harm.

I'm so proud of my son! – for all he has done –
and for all he continues to be!

He's a wonderful man – doing all that he can –
for his beautiful family!!

Though I see them just rarely –
I pray for them daily –
may the good lord (and Nonno!) look after –

And keep them safe and well –
with each dinner bell! –
'til we share our next meal and more laughter! :)

The Old Red Door

You can't tell a book by its cover
But you can tell a home by its door!
If red stands for passion and love –
Then that's what we painted it for!!

We didn't actually plan it
It's just the wife's favorite color
Red is so hearty and vibrant and warm –
To her – other colors seem duller!!

In the morning that door's pretty busy
Pop's all about moving cars –
In the night time the traffic just changes
To Marc – in and out with guitars!

Luke – with his music equipment
Also comes and goes – left and right
"Mr. Rizzo" – the teacher by day –
Becomes "Pony Boy" – D.J. by night!!

That red door was often the backdrop
For Marci-girl on a nice day
She'd set up her dolls on the front porch
With her girlfriends for hours she'd play.

Back then – neighborhood kids were abundant
There was always someone at the door –
"Of course you can come in and play!
That's what I opened it for!"

Any Sunday – if you should stop by
Just follow your nose through the door
The smell of red gravy on top of the stove
You'll be welcomed to dinner for sure!!

The more is the merrier on Sundays!
We can always squeeze in one more seat
Some red wine will perk up your taste buds!
For salad and pasta and meat!!

At holiday times and on weekends
The door's almost always unlocked –
(To the laundry room one might be streaking –
So announce yourself after you've knocked!!)

Other than that you are welcome
Anytime for some coffee or tea
Chicken soup – or for Friday night pizza
Always room for one more V.I.P.!

We carried our "Bundles of Joy" home
Through that repainted old red door
Not just once or twice were we blessed –
Brought new babies home twice again more!!

Now the wreath covered red door at Christmas
Opens up with excitement to greet –
Make way for Paul Jr. and wife and –
Pitter-patter of grandchildren's feet!!

Why if that old red door could just talk –
The stories would fill up a book!
Of weddings and parties and proms –
Where many a photo we took!

The door to our home is a haven
A lot of fond memories here
It opens and closes with love –
Year after year after year.

11–10–06

The Story of One 'Miracle-Michael' Rizzo
by Sister-in-Law Kathie
(based on Eulogy by beloved daughter Irene Simpson)

In a Jersey City tenement,
many years ago –
Lived a young and lovely bride Irene
and her handsome husband Joe.
Pregnant with her first-born
she accidentally fell –
Went into labor and gave birth
and things did not go well.

The baby appeared still-born –
he was wrapped and set aside –
The doctor was quite certain
that the little fella died.
But Grandma was attentive –
and saw the baby move –
She scooped him up – He gave a cry –
and the outcome did improve!

So little Michael Rizzo
was cherished from start –
This baby boy – this Miracle –
had won his family's heart!!
He grew to be a handsome man –
and went off to see the world –
In the Army and in Italy –
he met his favorite girl!

They both fell deeply so in love –
and after several dates –
Odette and he were married

and he brought her to the States.
They raised two kids in Jersey,
then to Florida they moved –
Through 55 years of marriage –
love and loyalty they proved!

They weren't rich or famous
or glamorous – and yet –
They left a Legacy of Love –
by the example that they set!

A simple man was Michael Rizzo –
He loved his family life –
He's fulfilled his earthly mission now –
reunited with his wife.

Smile when you think of him
and how he got his start –
And keep the lessons and his words
forever your heart! ...

"Thank God – that Grandma saved me! –
that she saw I was alive!
Or else I never
would have celebrated 85!! –
And never mind this crazy world –
the troubles and the rest! –
Just thank God that you were born –
and always try your best!!"

The one thing I remember most –
about this special guy –
He always said "I love you" –
before he said good-bye.

Antoinette

A bsolutely one of kind!!
N o one else can quite compare!
T otal devotion with family in mind
O vercoming hardship with care
I rresistable – her cooking and baking!
N ever encourage her singing!!!
E veryone agrees – No Mistaking!!!!
T hat singing is just NOT her thing!
T oday let us toast the 'ol gal —
E xpressing our friendship and love
      To our sister, wife, mother, & pal
         Strength and Grace —
            From Our Father Above.

Hey Cousin Mary Lou!

Hey cousin Mary Lou! – thanks for the evening!
And thanks for the dinner and gifts!!
What a great combination – family and food
I'm so grateful – my spirit uplifts!!!

It's always a pleasure – when we get together –
I hope we can meet again soon!
We don't need a birthday or special occasion
Let's not wait for another blue moon!!

You, me and Paul are now in our 60's!
So let's make the most of our years!!
How 'bout we do lunch or we take in a movie –
Now that we don't have careers!!!

Thanks once again for a wonderful meal
The cheesecake we won't be forgetting!!
Looking forward to seeing you next Saturday –
At Frankie and Judy's big wedding!!!!

Love always

B.F.F.

Who asks for so little
And gives so much more
Daily welcomes you home
When you walk through the door
Is always forgiving
When you're moody or cross
Will drop what he's doing
For a quick game of toss!

Who worships you just
For a romp in the park
Is content just to lay
By your feet in the dark
Who respects your opinion
When you're wrong or you're right
And alerts you to things
That go Bump – in the night!

Who's loving – and faithful
When you're up –
When you're down
Even longs to be near
When you're wearing a frown!

When the world seems against you
And you've nothing to spend –
Who'll still Love and Adore you?
Only Man's Best Friend!!

Love, Mom (Nov. 2004)

To Diane

I used to carry her on piggyback.
Still I picture us when looking back.
Through tangled time to vivid childhood.

On rainy days I'd take her on the bus
Side by side we'd sit, the two of us
Passing time. The world went whizzing by.

There was a time I thought she was like me
Another time I thought for sure she'd be
The last person to call me sister.

But here we are still sitting side by side
Still holding hands all through the rainy ride
Hold tight, the world's still whizzing by!

She's 50!!

It's Diane's 50th Birthday Bash
I'm happy you all are here
It's time now to offer the ol' girl a toast
So hold up your wine or your beer!

Here's to my younger kid sister
A reminder that I'm 50 PLUS!
We're the closest of all the Pell girls
My girdle's not tighter than us!!

We've shared through the years, our stories
Of how, why and where we came from
May I take this occasion to boast some
Of the Woman that she has become.

I recall her – the chubby cheeked toddler
I remember her beautiful teens
I admired the Strong Single mother
And she ALWAYS looked GREAT in her jeans!!!

A Waitress – a Singer/Masseuse
A Wedding Photographer she –
An Artist and Philosopher too
And – a lifelong Therapist – to me!!

For she is a Jolly Good Sister!
Three cheers for my very best friend!
Good Mother – Good Sister – Good Wife
Happy Birthdays be yours – without end!!!!

Pell Family Memories

I remember happy days in Waterloo
The country life – with lots for us to do
We climbed trees, caught pollywogs and snakes
Drive-in shows – and picnics at the lakes

Our "city mom" took up the farming life
A new role for the little Army wife
Who remembers – "Oh boy – squash again!"
Served up more than every now and then!!

We had sickle pears and vegetables galore
Mom never had to buy them at the store
Getting to our school was not too hard –
We simply had to walk across our yard!

And how about our trip to old Japan?
(On the way – we potty trained Diane!)
Went from Jersey to Frisco in our station wagon
With a mattress on the roof the whole time draggin'!

On the "U.S. Gaffy" we sailed forth
(Diane out of diapers – why of corth!)
We climbed decks and even saw some whales!
Mom kept hollering, "Don't go near the rails!!"

(Jim spent lots of time over the sink
Mostly throwing up is what I think
Mom was worried he might not survive
Despite his color – he managed to stay alive!)

Japan was an adventure for us all
Bamboo trees and rice paddies – recall
No heat in Sendai – in the mud we played
Dad brought home "Chiako" – our first maid!

Washington Heights in Tokyo was better
"Tokiko" was our maid – we can't forget her
With no TV we mastered cards and games
Read comic books – knew all the best one's names.

We came back on the "Mitchell" – then we flew
Back safely to our house in Waterloo
Dad got orders for West Point – My Heaven!
Mom broke her good news – 'bout # 7!!!

Back in Waterloo during that year
Is when we got our favorite dog so dear
We named him "Lashes" for his lovely eyes
Of all our dogs – He really was a Prize!

The best of homes I hope you'll all agree
Was West Point Military Academy!
There I spent the best years of my life
(Until becoming Paulie Rizzo's wife!!!)

'Twas there it was the good life that we found
With glorious scenic mountains all around
Swimming, skating, sports and Real Cadets!!
That's about as good as life can gets!!!

I know there's details that I am ignoring
One thing's for sure – Our life was never boring!!
Our share of happy memories are intact –
We're still the "Magnificent Seven" – That's a fact!!!

Writing While Riding...On a Train

I love my visits to VA –
Roger and Rosie are Great!
It's always a Beautiful stay –
Accommodations and food are First Rate!!
From the time I arrive at the station –
They welcome me into their home –
It's like a relaxing vacation! –
And the wine always sets the tone!!
Dinner's my favorite time –
Nice discussion and Rosie's cuisine!
Oh – and did I mention the wine? –
More mellow I have never been!!
It's a SPA – my visits with those two! –
It's such a calming retreat!
They even serve wine at lunch time! –
And finish the meal with a sweet!!
Then we all agree to a nap –
To their room retreat Roger and Rosie –
I start reading but in a snap –
I'm asleep 'cause the lounge is so cozy!!
Before you know it it's dinner –
And no matter what Rose Marie serves –
To be sure it's gonna be a winner!
With praises that she so deserves!!
And of course brother Roger keeps pouring! –
Our evening is mostly short-lived –
Before long we retire and are snoring! –
With dreams of what tomorrow will give!!
A good night's sleep and morning walk –
A start to the day that will please!
We share the newspapers with little talk –
Some hot coffee and toast with cheese!!

When I return back to New Jersey –
I'll cherish each pleasantry
I'll raise up my glass when I'm thirsty –
to Roger and Rosie and me!!!
He's an inspiration – my brother –
And Rose Marie also inspires!
He got only the best from our father and mother –
And Rosie fulfills his desires!
Beloved by his daughters and granddaughters too! –
What more can man really ask?
He accomplished in life more than most ever do –
With courage approaching each task!
May God continue to bless those two –
And their Beautiful family!
In good times and bad they have been True-Blue –
They are both such a treasure to me!!!

Bittersweet

Dear Saint Grandma 'Nello, how sweetly you lie,
Are you glad that I'm here? Do you mind if I cry?
Do you know how I love you? Remember my name?
It no longer matters – I love you the same.
Just to stand here beside you,
I'm filled with your grace.
I am happy and sad, when I look in your face.
I am filled with the memories
of you through the years.
A vision of love I can see through my tears.
The joy of your presence, Your voice and your smile,
We don't have to speak now, I'll just stay a while.

When I think of the things that you did and you said,
And of how I was loved, and of how I was FED! –
The stories you told, and the meals you prepared,
And the songs that you sang –
How you loved and you cared!
What can I do now for your love in return
But to stand here beside you
and touch you – and yearn
For the years that I had you beside me and then,
For Our Father to carry you home once again.
Dear Saint Grandma 'Nello How Fortunate I
To have known you – and loved you –
Do you mind if I cry?

Unsweetened!
(A Marriage Love Spat)

Oh my God! Look what you've done!!
You bought the wrong container!!!
I clearly wrote "unsweetened" –
but you went and bought the "plain-er!!!"
Can't you tell the red from blue?? –
no one drinks the plain!!
Tell me now – what will we do?!
Have you gone insane??!!

OK – OK I'll bring it back!
It just was a mistake!!
I couldn't find
"unsweetened" –
so the "plain" I thought I'd take!
I thought "plain" meant no sugar –
but I was clearly wrong –
Probably got distracted
'cause an old friend came along.

I'll go and get "unsweetened" –
no big deal! I'll bring it back!!
Not the point!! I wrote it down!!
What is it that you lack?
You've done this once before – you know –
and now you've done
It twice!! (Good thing you're keeping track –
so that I'll always pay the price!!)

I tried my very best (I thought) –
in following your list –
But I bought the wrong container –

and now you're really
Pissed!! I admitted I'm mistaken –
and I'll make another trip –
But the scolding doesn't end –
I must be punished for my slip!!

All the while I'm still cooking –
'cause we have to eat real
Soon – and the kids have heard your comments –
that I'm crazy
As a loon – so my appetite has dwindled –
and I'm feeling quite
Deflated – which cancels out this evening –
now that I have been berated.

All your noisy chastising –
'bout buying the wrong food –
Has diminished my libido –
you have really killed the mood.
So eat a bunch of chocolates –
for 'unsweetened' I must be!
(Though I shopped and made a nice meal –
didn't anybody see??)

Then called me back for dirty dishes –
such a charming fella!
Amused by your own antics –
while I feel like Cinderella.
Better get back to the store now –
(sure don't want another
Beatin') – no wonder I bought "plain" –
because they're out of the "unsweetened"!!

58

So I did some real quick thinkin' –
I had to wrack my brain!
What will he say if I tell him –
that they only had the "plain"?!!
So I scurried to the health food aisle –
and quickly said a
Prayer – thank you God – at last! –
I found "unsweetened" there

But wait! – I can do better! –
for I think I heard him utter
"Although it wasn't on the list –
you should have bought some butter!"
Back to the dairy aisle –
by the butter I am driven
If I can only get it right –
maybe I will be forgiven!

I wish I was a better wife –
and of course a better mother –
I never seem to get it right –
I'm thought of as a bother.
I should have gone to church –
For meditation and to pray –
Instead – catering to my family –
is how I spent my day.

Followed by a frantic quest –
to find the 'purple curtain' –
I promised my granddaughter
(she said "purple" – I am certain!!)
The day was left 'unsweetened' –
to my family I'm no winner –
– Except for sweet Andrea –

who I heard say, "Thanks for dinner."
Making me seem stupid –
in front of everyone – should not be a
Lesson for your daughter or your sons.
– What does it gain a man –
for the need to be so right?
Making mountains out of soy-milk –
and 'unsweetening' the night?!

Love anyways,
Thekath

Dear Paul

You really amaze me – truly you do!
You're a wonderful man – and I'll always love you.
Your abilities extend in every direction –
You're so generous with acts of your love and affection

You're dependable and loving and caring and strong –
So it's hard for me to tell you
when you have been wrong!
Not that anyone's perfect – it's too much to expect –
But when you make me feel stupid –
I'm totally wrecked!

If I say the wrong thing – it's not that it's planned –
You could nicely correct me – and I'd understand.
But instead you belittle and make me a fool!
Do I really deserve to be treated so cruel?

It's hard to take that from just anyone –
But from my own husband? –
and in front of our son??
Sometimes I don't know why I'm here or what for
When you put on that face –
I'm not sure anymore.

I don't want to be near you – or open my mouth
And we two become strangers in our very own house!
I am empty without you – I am crying inside –
Just a few angry words and I feel like I died.

You could have said sorry – but ignored it instead
So the tape of your words – repeats in my head.
It was just such a small thing – it was not a big deal!
And I must let it go – no matter how bad I feel.

You're the love of my life – you hold such a power –
Hold the key to my heart – every day every hour!
Why do I let you make me feel blue? –
is it what's wrong with me?
Or what's wrong with you?

Life's getting shorter for us both day by day –
So why be so hurtful in the things that we say? –
I need you to love me – understand and forgive –
Overlook and appreciate – for as long as we live!

To sum it all up – what I'm asking I guess –
Please make me feel valued – even when I'm a mess!
Please be patient with me – if I'm not always bright –
With so much on my mind – I can't always be right!

Do not undermine me – in my precious son's eyes!
It's not very manly to scold and chastise!!
Everything that I do – is with you in mind –
I don't consciously cross you! – so please just be kind.

For you are my man – and I am your wife –
And my heart's in your hands – for the rest of my life.
You mostly amaze me – truly you do! –
You're a wonderful man and I'll always love you.

To Natalie, From Mommy

It's the hardest thing I've ever had to do
To leave each day and say good-bye to you.
I miss your hugs and kisses and your smile
I'm at work – but thinking of you all the while.

My efforts now precede a better day
Still, I wish there was another way.
Enslaved by circumstances – I persist
Mindful of the moments that we've missed.

Steadfast is my focus on our dream
Prayerful that I won't run out of steam!
The vigil of your love burns in my heart
To keep me going while we are apart.

Your Grammy and your Grandpa love you so
Affording me the peace of mind to go.
With thoughts of you and them, I face the test –
And bow my head – and know that I am blessed.

Toasting and Roasting the Pop
On Approaching 60!!

Pop is gonna be 60!!!
It's hard to believe – but it's true!
We've come here together to roast him tonight
And he hasn't got even a clue!!!

Allow me to light up the fire
To let the roasting begin
No need for basting up this roast
Thanks to his oily Italian skin!!!!!

There's so much that I'd like to say
But since we haven't much time
I'll do the best I know how
By putting some thoughts into rhyme.

I remember the first time I saw him
He was short, dark and handsome for sure
At 'hello' he already had me
With those big brown eyes he did lure!

Soon we were blissfully married
Then in not much time at all
Mr. Short, dark and handsome – times two!
We welcomed another little Paul!!

We thought that we couldn't be happier
We so loved that cute little fella!
But the happiness so overcame us –
That along came our lovely Marcella!!

64

We were now just a perfect little family
But as soon as our Marci turned four –
We missed that 'new baby smell' so –
We decided – well maybe one more!

Thus then our little Marc joined us
Look at us now – we were five!!
Little did we ever imagine that
For one more kid we'd still strive!

Pop said that he hated odd numbers
So four would be better than three
We fixed up that problem with our Lukey
4 + 2 = 6 now were we!!!!!

Meantime Pop got a little involved
With school boards and coaching and such
Then got elected to the council
For volunteering – he just had the touch!!

By day he was out pushing drugs
To keep his wee family alive
By night he was all over Carlstadt
Running some raffle or drive!

But now he's a very proud grandpa
And all of the runnin' is done
He's still pushing drugs in the daytime –
To his family he's our number one!!!!!!!!!!

The best of all husbands and fathers
Keeps getting better each day
When we think he could not show more love
He manages to find a new way!!!!!!!

So Happy 60th Birthday Pop –
And 'Cient Ani' from all of us here
Let the roasting begin with a toast
So raise up your wine or your beer!!!!!

                    With all my love forever,
                    Kathie

My Son the Graduate

How does mother feel about her son
On Graduation Day?
Alive with the memories of her boy
That words cannot convey.

How do I speak of the joy that you brought
Even before your birth?
There isn't a scale of measure to show
The value of your worth.

You turned my life around, my son
That February sixth,
Confirming that Love and Marriage
Is more than just a myth.

Just at a time in my life
When I thought that my faith had dissolved,
God sent me you to believe in
And my doubts of His Love were resolved.

You'll never know how I love you
There's no way to know except one –
If the day comes when God will bestow upon you
A share in His Love, through a son. (Or Daughter!)

I'm SO PROUD of what you've accomplished!
So CONGRATULATIONS My Son!!
God bless you forever and keep you –
You'll always be my "Number One!!"

Love, Mom
1989

To My Dear Teenager (After an Argument)

I don't know why you choose to act this way
Your stubbornness can really spoil the day.
We have so little time that we can spend
And fighting only brings it to an end.

I work so very hard to show my love
And daily pray for wisdom from above.
To know just when I'm right and when I'm wrong
At times like this – I'm weakest when I'm strong.

There are so many things I do for you
Your laundry; pay the bills to name a few,
I don't expect you always to be sweet –
But when you leave this house, just please look neat!

To show my love for you because I care
I cleaned you – dressed you – groomed you –
fixed your hair.
I hoped that I had nurtured you inside
The attributes of self-love and of pride.

Maybe I overdid it when I fussed
But cleanliness and neatness is a must!
To love yourself as much now you must learn
And care about yourself – now it's Your turn.

Among the things I gave you through the years
The gifts I didn't buy are the most dear –
Be Kind; Be Faithful; Never Tell a Lie.
Hold on to those until the day you die.

Self-Love and Self-Respect hold value too
Remember them in everything you do.
Your treatment of the world will be its worst –
Unless you care about your own self first!

Love, Mom

To Marc with Love From Mom

I have loved you always
And I always will
Please let me tell you
Listen up and be still!

You have made me so happy
You have made me so proud
Since I don't tell you often
Let me shout it out loud!

I just want to protect you
Though I know you're a man
I say all the wrong things
Trying the best that I can.

It's so hard as a mother
To know what to do
When I know in my heart
Something's not right for you.

Should I just step aside
And not intervene?
Well mostly I do –
Not to make a big scene.

This time I can't do that
I just had to find out
If my intuitions were valid
And what my worries were about.

You know that I'm busy
With so much to do
I'm not looking for trouble
But because I love you –

I questioned your brothers
And Sister-in-law too
They didn't want to answer
But I insisted they do.

I couldn't ignore it
Though I knew you'd be mad
Still I had to confront you
–A Whole Week I've Been Sad!

I know you love music
And music loves you!!
But life's not that simple
To your own self BE TRUE!!

There are good times and bad times
For the rest of your life
Use your Heart and your Mind
To handle your strife!!

I pray every night
And I pray every day
But it's really up to you
To find the best way.

Dear God keep them safe
Mother Mary – Please guide them
Give them Courage and Wisdom
And an Angel beside them!!

Do I make any sense?
Do I come on too strong??
Am I going too far?
Are my instincts all wrong???

Sometimes the truth
Is a real bitter pill
But – I have loved you Always
And I Always will.

Love, Always, Mom 2004

Off My Chest

The truth of the matter is this
I was waiting downstairs for a kiss
I just couldn't think
I had too much to drink!
And got stuck in a moment of bliss.

How I waited for Saturday night
To dance in your arms holding tight
The fault was all mine
I had way too much wine!
The last thing I wanted was to fight.

Negativity plays like a tape
In my head so I look to escape
I count on romance
And for our next dance
That's where my fantasies take shape.

I guess I'm a dreamer – a fool!!
(Which is why I remain still in school)
Why else do I rhyme
And waste so much time?
I must be as dumb as a mule!

Your patience with me has worn thin
Too often I feel I can't win.
Everything is just fine
When I'm walking the line
But to err – is a big mortal sin!!

I guess what I'm trying to say
Is I wish you could just find a way
To be extra kind
Instead of blowing my mind
With your criticisms of me every day.

And what would it cost – what's the price?
Sometimes to say I look nice
(You could have last night –
Am I such a bad sight??)
A compliment sure can entice.

I'd Love you to kiss me hello
I Need your affection to show
Some Tenderness display
Go ahead – Make my day!
Only You have the Power you know!!

Or maybe we're married so long
That you no longer sing me that song
But it sure does feel good
And I wish that you would
It might keep things from turning out wrong.

All my love, Kathie
03-13-05

Empty Nest

You ask if I can always write a poem
The answer's yes – when mostly I am home
There's stuff inside of me needs to come out
The pen relieves – so I won't have to shout!

I guess I'm needy for someone to hear
So often there is no one really near
(They barely notice – even when they are
It seems they like me best when I am far!)

I thought somewhere along that we would bond
Of our relationship – they'd remain fond
Instead to fill my time I'm always looking
They only come around if I am cooking!

I felt so close, connected – loved so strong
I guess I'll never know just what went wrong
I fell off the golden pedestal I guess
I work so hard – but can't clean up my mess.

All of my kids have Really Made Me Proud
I never miss the chance to say out loud!
So in my heart I know did them right
Still I miss their love – both day and night

I used to hug and kiss them all the time
Sang songs and taught them every nursery rhyme
We read stories and we even liked to bake
So where exactly was my big mistake?

I ran them everywhere they had to go
And showed up almost every game and show
We went swimming everyday in Capo's pool
I stayed home from work 'til Luke had started school

I realize they have lives of their own
And sometimes I get calls now on the phone
I guess I really long for an embrace
Or just a smile when they see my face.

I'm always glad to see them when they come
When they were little – home to me they'd run
Filled with stories of their day and lots to tell
They hardly speak now – since off my throne I fell.

Oh well – there's still a lot for me to do
Guess I'll go back to school – Learn something new
I'll teach my dance – or maybe write a poem
And pray I'm here the next time they come home.

2004

The Magnificent Seven

FAMILY REUNION 2001

On the 12th of August, in 2001
The "Magnificent Seven" all gathered for fun.
There was Roger and Rosie and Keith and Kristina –
The Little "Big Sister" and the sweet new Bambina!!
Two sisters so cute from their heads to their toes –
Lovely Francesca and now Abigail Rose!!
Who knew there'd be grandkids in 2001?!
Even Kevin and Dorothy and Dennis, their son –
Have "gone forth and multiplied" –
and not just by one!
Dennis and Pam have kept up the cycle –
With adorable Miranda and cute little Michael!!
(Connie and Roger must have beamed from above–
Seeing their children all gathered in love.)

Even Jim and Diana and Jennifer and Lee!
All flew in from Cal. To join the party!!
Jen's Such a Beauty – and Lee's Such a Cook!!
(With 2 blondes in the family –
not so Italian we look!!)
What a blessing to all that they made the flight –
Their presence So Special made everything Right!
Young Kevin and Dorothy and Brian all brought
Boyfriend and girlfriends
(and Good-Looking we thought!!)
To see them all grown-up —
So Handsome and Pretty –
(3 Serious Policemen – and Dorothy – So Witty!!)
How in this world that seems practically Mad –
Did we all get so lucky with the kids that we had?!

We Must have done Some things
that turned out all right
For to see Such Fine people was Such a Good Sight!!
Kathie and Paul with 2 of their 4 –
(Marci was away and Marc was on tour.)
But young Paul brought Kristin
and Luke brought his Janet
(So hard to get 'em all,
no matter how well you plan it!)
But all 4 of our kids have made us both proud –
In the true Pell tradition – They stand out in a crowd!
A Musician, a Teacher, a Student and a Dean
(Of course Paul thinks
it's the Rizzo tradition that's seen!)

Moving on to the folks who came here from Spain
9 hours all squooshed on an overcrowded plane!
That Connie and Marce – They're Such a Great Pair!
We were So Glad to see them –
So Glad they were there!!
So Sorry that Sabi and Lou couldn't come–
Working Summers for college is not always fun.
What a couple Of Great Kids they are – by the way!
We hope they'll come visit us soon one fine day.
As it was – Lou's appendix decided to Burst!
Thank God – he's OK – for it could have been worse.
Connie's family and friends all took very good care –
Not to let on to Connie 'til they returned there.
Connie and Marce couldn't believe their own eyes –
Lou met them at the airport with his news of surprise.
"So what did you do while we were away son?"
"Oh not very much – Just had an operation."

78

"What?!!!!" Connie said –
as he showed them his scar –
She darn almost Fainted – but she didn't fall far.
Lou caught her and assured them that he was OK –
Now he's studying in Valencia –
Whew! What more can we say?
And Sabi – that Angel – never said on the phone –
Careful not to upset them and make them rush home.
By his bedside she bravely took care of her brother,
Taking the place of her father and mother.
Like I said – We've Been Blessed
by the Great Kids we've raised –
Though they give us grey hairs –
They at times should be praised!!!!
To Barcelona to study – Sabi now has returned
Taking with her, the lessons
as Nurse she has learned!!
(We hope you're both safe while you are away –
And look forward to seeing you again here someday.)

Getting back to the reunion of 2001 –
Did I mention Dear Diane and her Wonderful Son?
Our Photographer Sister and the Talented Ben!
(How can I do justice with just this old pen?!)
Hats off to Diane for her hard work that day!
Taking pictures of all – in her ARTISTIC way.
For her efforts in planning
in the weeks that preceded –
Making sure the arrangements
covered all that we needed.
To make for a day that was PERFECTLY GRAND!
From the steak to the cake –
How much food could we stand??!!

And the food never stopped –
We Pells Do Like To Eat!!!!
We were happy that Jimmy and Arlene could be there
And Crissy and Kids – And our Dearest Aunt Mare!!
When we say to Aunt Mary – Long Live the Queen!
We Love You Like Crazy – is all that we mean.
That we all got together – It just means So Much –
Let's all Stay together by keeping in touch.
The First Pell Reunion turned out to be GREAT!
For the next one to happen – Not too long let us wait!!

In the meantime let's keep up our family ties –
With lots of hellos – instead of good-byes.
The Family Reunion – 2001 –
PROOF that we Pells still know how to have FUN!!

God Bless Us Everyone!
Love, Kathie Rizzo (and Paul!)

To Paul

My husband's eyes are round and dark
His smile is warm and ready
His fingers square and capable
His touch is soft but steady.

Although he's not a wealthy man
You'd never even guess
A spender and a giver
He's a man most generous.

He fills me when I'm near him
I'm empty when he's far
The universe is plentiful
But he's my shining star.

I love to walk beside him
In his presence I am whole
He gives my life direction
And leads me to my goal.

My husband's eyes are round and dark
His smile could melt my heart
My love is his forever
As I loved him from the start.

July 1988

81

Angelina Grace

Soft as a rosebud
With cheeks of peachy-pink
Hair all dark and shiny
Like satin – silk – or mink!

Eyes that dance and sparkle
From ear to ear – a smile
Pretty as a picture and –
Always dressed in style!

Delightful and good natured
Irresistible her laugh
Enjoying every moment
Eating – playing – and the bath!

Artists have attempted to
Depict an angel's face
But none can hold a candle
To our Angelina Grace!!

July 2005

Angelina Turns 18!

With lots of love and good wishes and blessings from
above, from Nonno & Nonna

Eighteen happy years ago
you came into our lives!
You set your family's hearts aglow –
and strengthened your parents' ties.

What a woman you've become! –
looking back we smile and sigh –
Dear granddaughter our number one! –
it's a joy to watch you fly!

You've been the greatest sister –
to Gigi and your brothers!
A coffee shop barista –
who plays piano like no others!!

Mature and so responsible!
You've come so very far –
A young adult most capable! –
even driving your own car!!

We recall your childhood –
as 'mother's little helper' –
Doing all the things you should –
for your family's care and welfare.

You've always stayed a good girl –
and set a good example!
Pure and shining as a pearl! –
and careful not to trample.

Looking out for others' needs
with cheerfulness and grace!
Demonstrating Christian deeds –
with that lovely smiling face!! :)

Our birthday wish comes in a prayer –
from New Jersey and from heaven :)

God our heavenly father above –
keep Angelina in your care!
Please always fill her life with love –
by the light of your presence there.

Protect her from all evil! –
and steer her from temptation!
Help her recognize the devil! –
who never takes vacation!!

May she follow with precision –
let your love-light lead the way –
With clear conscience and clear vision –
in the night and every day!

By your teachings and your guidance –
and a family love so strong –
Please keep Satan at a distance –
and let this woman not do wrong.
But always by her side remain –
even when the going gets rough!
Let always her faith in you sustain –
your presence will be enough!
Oh – and one more thing to end this prayer –
I promise to be short –

We thank you our creator –
for our Angelina Grace!
She couldn't be much greater! –
that lovely smile and that face!!
You really wrapped her up just right –
she's such a special gift!
She's such a lovely soul – not just a lovely sight! –
so never let her go adrift – her family loves her so!!

(Especially Nonno and Nonna!)
Happy 18th birthday dear Angelina!!
Xoxoxoxoxoxoxoxoxox

Along Came Camila Irene!

Along came baby Camila –
a timely and welcome surprise!
With abundant and curly black hair –
and melt-your-heart big brown eyes!!
She's Sofia's little sidekick –
a perfect fit as the little sis –
Spilling over with loads of love and affection –
ever-ready with a hug and a kiss!!
She keeps all her family laughing! –
with her antics, expressions and tricks –
Encouraged by Sofi's enjoyment –
will entertain everyone just for kicks!!
There's a mutual admiration –
that binds them in sisterly love –
Such a beautiful intimate devotion –
can only come from heaven above.
So move over Elsa and Anna! –
these sisters are authentic and sweet!
The 'real deal' – not a couple of Disney girls –
so don't even try to compete!!
Little sister's a force to be noticed –
though she's still a newcomer on the scene –
But Sofi stepped up as a 'big sister' –
when along came Camila Irene!
God bless these two Rizzo sisters –
may they always remain side by side –
Camila Irene you're a blessing to us all! –
we love you with hearts open wide!!

With Love to Landon on Your 13th Birthday

I can't believe that now you are thirteen –
The years have flown so very fast!
We watched you grow through visits in-between –
Our hopes and expectations you've surpassed!

As a young man and a Christian comes the test –
The challenges you'll face still lie ahead –
With precious family love you have been blessed!
Now follow in the path that Jesus led!

Find a need and fill it – best you can!
When others take the low road – you go high!
Money and fine things don't make the man –
The best in life – money still can't buy!

It's 'faith and love and charity' –
That marks us in the end –
"The greatest being love" – said He
For both enemy and friend!

Now, that message is really tough! –
But with God's grace you'll manage!
When you find that life gets rough –
Trust in faith as your advantage!

Tears and fears are part of life!
Don't be ashamed to share!
Everyone has stress and strife!
Reach out with love and prayer!

When given the choice to 'be right' or 'be kind' –
Let Jesus be your light!
Sometimes we need to put ego aside –
Know that 'kind' is more godly than 'right'!

Well there you have it dear grandson!
With love and with pride I convey –
In addition to being so smart and handsome –
May you grow in God's goodness I pray!

From Nonna and Nonno too :) 5-22-22 xoxoxoxoxo

Our Gianna Lynn

GIANNA LYNN — with the curly-curls —
One of our favorite little girls!
Face of a cherub —
A huggable hug —
A huggable honeybunch —
Cute as a bug!

A JOY to her sister —
DELIGHT to her brother —
A SURPRISE and a BLESSING –
For her father and mother!

Sparkling eyes —
And an elfin grin —
A HEAVENLY GIFT —
Our GIANNA LYNN!!

With Lots of Love and Hugs,
        Nonna and Nonno – August 2011

Our Boy Braxton

Our boy Braxton, who just turned three –
is quite a little man!
He hasn't quite mastered
all the 'Team Rizzo' skills –
But he's sure out to prove that he can!!

His energy is endless! – his antics are fearless!
In his play he is brave and he's bold!
He's a match and a challenge
to his brothers and sisters –
And yet, he is just three years old!!

He's a real firecracker and so full of spunk! –
Never runs out of fuel or gets tired!
Makes the most of each day –
hard at work in his play –
With four siblings to keep him inspired!

He keeps everyone on watch and on lookout –
For daily he learns and tries something new –
Yet, loving that boy
Braxton comes so easy –
It doesn't hurt that he's quite handsome too!!

He's a handful – but he is a blessing!
Hide the cookies – or he'll eat them all!!
Our boy Braxton
can get into mischief at times! –
(He takes after his father Paul!) :)

We love him to pieces 24-7 – he fills up our lives with
joy!
God only knows –
he keeps us all on our toes! –
But he's a 'keeper' – he's Braxton our boy!!!

Love Nonna! 12–25–19

Happy First Birthday Thorin!

Baby Thorin Thomas
is our newest family member!
He joined the happy Rizzo Team
on the 18th of December.

With Love and Joy was welcomed
by his Father and his mother –
The favorite Christmas present
to his sisters and his brother!

A handsome little peanut
with the biggest, brownest eyes!
Good looks run in his family –
so it's really no surprise!!

Surrounded by his siblings –
he is such a precious sight –
They lavish him with kisses
every morning, noon and night!

His parents share a special bond
that's based on Faith and Love,
Empowering their devotion
with wisdom from above.

Blessed with siblings,
aunts and uncles and cousins, so far 4 –
And the lucky little 'Peanut Boy' –
has grandparents galore!

His household's always jumping –
with pretend dinosaurs a-roarin'!
With piano songs and make believe –
It's like Disneyland for Thorin!!

Let prayer reflect our gratitude –
and when the day is done –
Let's give thanks for Baby Thorin –
God has blessed us everyone!!

With Lots of Love,
Nonna & Nonno & Uncle Marc

Happy 3rd Birthday Sofia!!

SOFIA LUCIANA RIZZO –
sent down from Heaven above!
On October 14, 2010 –
A gift of God's Grace and Pure Love!!

She wiggled and screamed on the table —
where the nurses attended with care.
As if Radiant Beauty wasn't enough —
she made sure that we noticed her there!

Oh what a Glorious moment in time —
the Beautiful day of her birth!!
An Aura of Family Love filled the room —
to her parents – a New Hope and Worth!

And for every day since and thereafter —
Love rules the world once again!
The Joyful Sofia came into our hearts! –
Who remembers a life before then??

On this her 3rd Birthday I'm writing this poem —
to acknowledge, celebrate and include
The AWESOMENESS of our Creator God! –
With a prayer of Sincere Gratitude!

So Happy 3rd Birthday Sofia! –
You're the Pride of your whole family!
God Bless You and Keep you Forever from harm —
Is the prayer that we pray constantly

With Lots of Love and Prayers Always,
Nonna and Nonno and Uncle Marc

3. TEACHING

Kindergarten ABCs
by Mrs. Rizzo

A is for Applesauce we made in September
B is for Beautiful Fall
C is for Carving our pumpkin together
D is for Decorating the hall
E is for Everyone's growing
Faster than you can say — BOO!
G is the Growth that we measured
H is for "How tall are you?"
I is for Inches that show us
Just who is tall and who's not
K is for Kindergarten children
L is for Learning a Lot!
M is for Math. Everyday
N is for Numbers are Neat!
O is for Over and Over
Patterns repeat and repeat!
Q is for Quickly and Quietly
R is for learning to Rhyme
S is for Safety when we're on the Stairs
T is for Taking our Time
U is for Unbelievable news!
V is for Very nice shades
W is for Wonderful new Windows!!
'Xcellent improvements were made!!!
Y is for Yes — we love school!
Z— We took off with a Zoom!
To see for yourself what we're up to
Just visit the Kindergarten room!!

Much To Do in March

March came in like a lion,
The weather was snowy and cold.
The children spotted a Leprechaun
In their class — with a pot of gold!

They all took a guess at how many
Gold coins he had in his pot —
Then recorded their estimations;
They could see that there were a lot!

Counting the coins came next
TO find out the actual number.
First by 10's — then by 5's — then by 2's —
Practicing helps them remember!

On Healthy Snack Day they learned
That by cutting an apple or pear
Into halves or into quarters,
Their friends could have a "fair share".

Sharing with friends is such fun!
They had apples and bagels and cheese.
The children all showed their good manners, —
They always say "Thank you" and "Please."

The school nurse was there to explain
How important it is that they eat,
Mostly all good healthy foods
With just an occasional treat.

"Finding Nemo" continues to flourish!
The fish are all swimming along.
For the children whose parents share reading —
Their reading skills are growing strong!

In March there is still much to do,
Like counting the days down 'til Spring!
Enjoying the stories of Dear Dr. Seuss –
And wondering what the bunny will bring!!

April in Kindergarten

While showers bring flowers
We've been working for hours
Making colored eggs for finding
And kites for unwinding!

Baby animals grow up
Like a dog from a pup
We brought baby pictures for showing
Just how much <u>we</u> are growing!

We saved milk cartons and then
We recycled them again
As a home for our seeds
It's what our earth needs!

In the darkness of night
With our scientist's flashlight
To the stars we did zoom
In our own A.P. room!

It was so very cool
To bring bunnies to school
Even "Dexter"– The live one
Made Bunny Day – such fun!

Busy birds in the trees
In our class – "busy bees"
Kindergarten's exciting
We are reading and writing!

Springtime in Kindergarten!

It's Springtime in Kindergarten!
What is going on?
Creative Spring activities
Now that Winter's gone.

Ladybugs and flowers
Blossoms on the trees
Baby chicks and bunnies
Butterflies and bees —

Pastel patterned chains
Of yellow, pink and blue
The handiwork of children
Who love to cut and glue!

Springtime in Kindergarten!
A time to watch things grow
The students planted flowers
(It's Science, as you know.)

The windowsills are lined up
With containers growing seeds –
Sunlight – air and water —
All living things have needs.

Springtime in Kindergarten'
Come and take a look!!
The rug's a perfect place
For little friends to share a book.

Or at the tables
Writing sentences
Preparing for first grade
(All the lovely decorations –
Are by kindergarten made!)

Springtime in Kindergarten!
Chocolate treats and jellybeans!!
Hiding eggs around the classroom –
What the happy season means!

Sorting by the colors –
And tallies on the graph –
Sharpen up the thinking skills
For "Everyday Math!!"

Yes! It's Springtime in Kindergarten!
There's still a lot to do –
Like class trips and Field Day –
And Graduation too!!!

By Mrs. Rizzo April 2006

The Seasons of Kindergarten

It's hard to remember —
way back in September
When the children just started school
They struggled with laces —
and made funny faces
While trying to follow each rule.

In October, November, –
and right through December
They recited each Nursery Rhyme
As they mastered each letter —
they got better and better
And even learned how to tell time!

Then came the New Year —
The lessons became clear
The rules and routines were down pat
Math journals got done —
Celebrations were fun
Especially "The Cat in The Hat!!"

After Spring vacation —
they visited the Police Station
Before that — a trip to the Library
The Children's Museum is soon —
Then before long it's June
How fast went this year? — Oh —My — Very!!!!

Now the reading is stronger —
Their sentences longer
The writing — So Neat on the Lines!
In addition, subtraction —
and other Math action
It's Amazing how Kindergarten Shines!!

Looking back on the seasons —
there are so many reasons
To applaud what a Great year they've had!
The memory of class trips —
puts a smile on their lips
And then Summer! — A time to be glad!!!!!!!

By Mrs. Rizzo – May 2007

Starting School

Today I woke up early
It's my first day of school –
Mommy served me pancakes and
Everything is cool!

Friends are waiting for me
Outside by my door –
Remember to blow kisses
Till I'm home again once more!

Summertime has ended
They covered up the pool –
Having fun with friends now
Over in my school!

On my way to Kindergarten to
Learn how to read and write –
And I'll tell you all about it
When you tuck me in tonight!

Healthy Snacking in Kindergarten

Healthy foods are good to eat
Grapes and berries – oh so sweet!
Juicy oranges and tasty pears
Packed in a lunchbox by someone who cares!!

Peanut Butter and crackers to munch
Yogurt before or after lunch!
Crunchy celery and carrot sticks
With cream cheese and raisins – makes a nice mix!!

Veggies with a yummy dip
Water or fruit juice — nice to sip!
Some drink milk to make them strong
With healthy snacks — you can't go wrong!!

Cookies and cakes are for a party
Everyday snacks should be healthy and hearty!
Forget the donuts, chips and candy
Bananas and apples are oh so handy!!

Hard boiled eggs — nuts — pretzels — cheese
Applesauce — peaches — or pineapples please!
Junk food is such an unhealthy habit
And makes some kids jump around like a rabbit!!

So on the weekends — plan ahead
Put healthy snacks in the lunchbox instead!
From nutritious snack foods — your child can choose
With good health habits — you just can't lose!!

I Love Reading!

I love to read
I read every day
Sometimes at recess
I give up my play!

I read to my teachers
Because it's such fun
When I finish one book –
I start another one!

I read with expression
As I turn every page
And I'll keep right on reading
No matter what age!

Because reading is fun
And it makes me so smart
And the stories I read
Will live on in my heart!

For I love to read
Springtime, Winter or Fall
But Summertime reading
I like best of all!!

So I'll visit the library
To read where it's cool
I'll be smarter than ever
When I come back to school!!

Kindergarten Class Trip

The Children's Museum
Is a wonderful place –
Imagination illuminates
On each child's face.
Pretend you're a Doctor
Or an Astronaut,
Ballerina, Musician –
There is quite a lot
You can do there for fun
While you learn so much –
And there isn't a sign
That says, "Do Not Touch."

Be a Cowboy – or girl
Ride a horse, "Giddyap!"
Catch a fish with a pole –
Read a big wall map.
Wear costumes and act
Out "The Three Little Pigs" –
Or head to the Sandbox
For Dinosaur digs!
In the Post Office
You can deliver the mail –
Serve up lunch in the Deli –
Or spend time in a Jail!!

Be a Weather Reporter
Or pretend you're a Dentist
Experiment and observe –
Like a real Scientist!

The best part of all
Is to be with your friends
Learning – "hands on"
Where the fun never ends!
The perfect ending
Is a picnic lunch –
And a real School Bus ride
With the whole happy bunch!!

By Mrs. Rizzo – May 2005

Nature-Watch

J ust in time for Winter –
A utumn shook the leaves!
N ow the squirrels' nests we see —
U p high in the trees!!
A nimals need shelter from
R ain and wind and snow —
Y ou and I are warm here in our houses down below!

Mrs. Rizzo – Jan. 2008

We Do So love That Dr. Seuss!!

That Dr. Seuss! That Dr. Seuss! —
We do so love that Dr. Seuss!!
Still makes us laugh time after time —
just using silly words in rhyme!
He exercised imagination —
to formulate his own creation!
The "King of Nonsense" (so to speak) —
invented characters so unique!
And crazy creatures of all sizes —
to fill his stories with surprises!!

What a nuisance in a Hat —
was that nasty naughty Cat!
No cat ever acted ruder —
than that red striped Hat intruder!!
Made a house the scene of crime —
then fixed it in the nick of time!
Now who could think up such abuse? —
The one and only — Dr. Seuss!!
He wrapped it all up cleverly —
a clever wrapper-upper he!!!

He tamed our wildest, weirdest dreams —
with zany and preposterous schemes!
Granted the Grinch a happy ending —
a Masterpiece of story-bending!!
That Dr. Seuss! That Dr. Seuss!! —
Doused our worst fears on the loose!
Transforming them for ever-after —
in illustrated tales of laughter!
We do so love that crafty man! —
Thank you, thank you 'Sam I Am!!'

We "Baby Boomers" way back read —
the Seuss books on our couch and bed!
With a fox or with a goat —
we laughed at everything he wrote!
By politics and war we're wracked! —
Our sense of humor's still intact!!
We Seussed our offspring and their kids —
It saved us all from 'flipping lids'!
From the "Guru of Giggles" —
HOPE has flowered! – By his pages we're
EMPOWERED!!

Each book is a written prescription —
a dose of the Doctor's hilarious fiction!
Prescribed by the good ol' Doctor himself! —
A quick-fix for all on the library shelf!!
Need a 'pick-me-up'? – a lift – or a boost?? —
Just grab a copy and get yourself Seussed!!
You'll feel lighter! Feel even better –
reading a Seuss-book with someone together!!
We do so love that Healthy-Healer!
That funny-bone-tickling-Good-Mood-Dealer!!

Especially in a classroom crowd —
his books make students laugh out loud!
Teachers depend on him tried and true —
to regroup — refocus – release and renew!!
A lively Seuss-book intermission —
unclogs brains from fractions and friction!!
Reading for fun provides many uses —
Just turning pages untightens the nooses!!!
(In a mental-health journal –
I think I once read it —

or maybe the good Doctor Seuss
even said it!)
Either way to fight stress
it's a healthy solution!
Recycling his books even limits
Pollution!

These lessons on pages –
will pass down through the ages –
Eat your Green Eggs and Ham –
in a taxi, or tram!
In a box with a fox –
or without any socks!!
Some days we don't get it –
like when we first read it –
Re-read it again –
this time to a kid! –
A kid will start laughing
just like we once did!!

We'll be tickled I think –
We'll be tickled quite pink!
We'll laugh to and fro –
and we'll feel our hearts grow!!
By the end of the book –
we'll take on a New Look!
It feels good to let loose –
Thanks again Dr. Seuss!!
(But the question remains
as this poem is complete –
What really happened
on Mulberry Street??)

Holiday Thank You Card

A great big thank you!
From me to you
For making holiday
Dreams come true!!

When I got home
I had such fun –
Opening cards and presents
One by one.

I love the jewelry –
The cookies and candy –
Candles and Santa pillow –
Sure came in handy!!

The lotions and lipsticks
And pretty perfume
I put on my dresser
At home in my room!

A gingerbread house!
And a nice travel set!! –
Notepaper and salad bowls!
How lucky can I get!!

Some soaps for the bath –
And a beautiful doll! –
And a nice visa gift card
To spend at the mall!!

If the weather reporters
Predict a snow storm –
With my new winter scarves
I'll be cozy and warm!!

Your gifts and good wishes
Brought joy – it is true!
But mostly I'm thankful
For each one of you!!!!

Here's wishing you all peace, happiness and health in
2008

Bergenfield's Best

What will we do without Diane Olson?
How will we ever endure??
A master of all trades – and then even more-some
A tough act to follow – <u>for sure!</u>

It's just not the same without Diane,
Her smile is gone from the hall –
We're carrying on here – the best that we can –
But we'll miss her when Autumn leaves fall.

Who'll train the "safeties" – and count every penny?
Collect for the raffles – and more?
Who can replace her? There just aren't any!
To fill her position – will take <u>four!!</u>

To tell why she's missed – there are too many reasons,
Her bright eyes – her bright smile – and her laughter!
I guess you could call her "A Teacher for All Seasons"
And her light will shine on – ever after!

She never surrendered to tired or weary –
A woman <u>with</u> <u>spunk</u> – on the go!
Would have stayed in the race, with her attitude
cheery –
Were it not for a troublesome toe!

May God bless the Lady in <u>Penn</u>-sy
And we hope that she'll often come back
Remembering that Bergenfield she <u>can</u>–see
Just a stone's throw from old Hackensack!

2004

115

Bye-Bye Bergenfield

Bye-bye Bergenfield friends!
Thanks for a very good run!!
I'll miss the memories made here –
Especially the laughter and fun!!!

You've all been a great bunch to work with!
I'll never forget your support!!
Always willing to lend me a hand –
With the computer when I came up short!!!

I especially want to acknowledge
The gals from the Primary wing –
Who listened at lunch and traded ideas –
And shared just about everything!

Bear with me now as I name them –
Starting with a fine lass like Deirdra!
So helpful and cheerful, lighthearted and kind –
Here's to the good folks that reared ya!!

Moving along on the roster –
Next to the Linda's I'll switch!
In alphabetical order I'll go –
So you won't have to ask which is which?!

Making house-calls from up on the 3'd floor
That would have to be "new" Linda G.!
A.M. and P.M. my sidekick and friend
None other than the "old" Linda T.!!

And last but not least of the Linda's —
"The Iditarod" might be a clue –
Or stocking the Bergenfield Pantry –
You guessed it — "First Grade" Linda Q.!!!

Down the hall are my friends Pat and Krissy –
Each on the spot with their smiles!
One keeping up with the Yankees –
And one keeping up with the styles!!!

And Maura – whose loyal assistance
Helped me launch each September with ease!
Guarding the doors to prevent an escape –
Making the first days a breeze!!!

Candice is "the new kid on the block" –
You've already made an impression!
With the wonderful vibes that I'm getting –
You're a credit to the teaching profession!!

And way down at the end of the hall –
With Kerri it was plain from the start –
That Washington School inherited a gem! –
A pearl-of-a-girl with a heart!!!!

May I be the first to commend you –
For forthcoming tenure — earned twice!
A shining example of greatness –
Your technique and presence — so nice!!!

Then there's Robin and Linda T. and Fran –
Who frequent my classroom a lot! —
Offering a shoulder or ear to rely on –
And solutions right on the spot!!!

For all kinds of coverage that I'll call
'Miscellaneous' – No one can beat 'em –
Helping kids on computers and such –
And bathroom breaks just when I need 'em!!!

God bless you for always providing
Me with all kinds of 'stuff' that I'm needing –
Like Therapy — Encouragement — and Laughter –
Even came to my Poetry Reading!!!!!!!!!!!!!

In singing the praises of co-workers –
I can't overlook our fine staff!
Such as Nancy — our well-dressed Secretary!
With whom I've shared many a good laugh!!

With Custodial Experts on board –
Like Victor and Rick and Glen –
No wonder our building runs smoothly!
Under careful control of such men!!

I thank God for my 2nd floor friends –
Like Nancy and Donna and Tam!
Who regularly rescue me from –
The copy machine in a jam!!!

2008

Ode to Sister Marigene

How does your Faculty love you?
Let us count the ways.
First thing every morning
You fortify our days.

You stir our minds and spirits
To keep us at our best.
To have you as our leader
We feel that we are blessed.

Your ready sense of humor
Is written on your face.
We love it when you tell us that
You want to "just touch base."

First Fridays come so quickly
And when we see your cards
We know it's time for business
(Though we'd rather be on Mars!)

At times your temper's tested
But you count to ten instead.
We've never seen you "lose it"
(Just once your face turned red.)

We're honored when you praise us
But please make no mistake –
The thing we most appreciate –
Is when you bring us cake!!

I guess by now you've noticed
We're not a somber bunch.
We'd hide it if we could but –
You've been with us at lunch!

We know that you accept us
And on a serious note –
Your presence here among us
Has kept us all afloat.

We thank you most sincerely
For your love and expertise.
Like The One you chose to follow –
You're a message of His Peace.

God bless you Sister Marigene
For everything you do.
Be assured our prayers today –
Are especially for You.

Here Comes Mrs. Mendelsohn

You are SUCH a Wonder!
You are SUCH a Delight!
When you enter our classroom
You're a REAL welcome sight!!

Using actions and puppets!
And piano and guitar!!
Did you learn that in college –
Or were you just born a Star?!!

We're SO LUCKY to have you
You spice up our day!
With your singing and dancing –
And movement and play!

You're SO Gifted and Talented
You could have been Famous!
If the world ever finds out –
They'll probably blame us!

For keeping the secret
Of our own Mrs. M.
But why should we share with the world
Such a GEM?!

"Could have been a contender!"
But instead you are here –
The children of Bergenfield
All give you a Cheer!!!!!

We're SO Glad you chose us –
We're SO Happy you did!
You are Truly a Blessing
For each Teacher and Kid!

Hope your own family knows
Of the MAGIC you bring!
You EMPOWER our children
When you teach them to sing!

Always full of surprises
Bringing something that's new –
When they give out the Grammys — They should give
one to YOU!

2003

The One and Only – Joan Gunther!!

There is only one "Miss Gunther"
Soft and Cuddly – Brave and Bold!
The Good Lord made her Special –
Then He threw away the mold!!

Her classroom is Eclectic
It's Unique – One of a Kind!
She's got a Dancing Bunny –
That will really blow your mind!!

– And all kinds of Cool Equipment
Animated Visual Aids!
If you've never been to Guntherland –
Prepare to be Amazed!!

When it comes to storytelling
Eat your heart out Mother Goose!
No one wears the Striped Hat better
Not even Doctor Seuss!!

If something strikes her funny
Her laughter is Contagious!
When she's reading to her class
Her Voices are Outrageous!!

While passing by her room
You might think that she is Wacky!
Until you realize –
She's just imitating "Tacky!!"

Full of Effervescent Fun
Always looking to Make Merry!
Out to Dine and Wine with Friends –
Or Twirling Weekends with her Sherry!!

She kept up with her studies
There was nothing that could stop her!
Remember Our Surprise –
When we found out she was – A Doctor!!

The Jewel of Lindbergh School

A few inspired words about a lady —
That all of Carlstadt knows as MRS. GRADY!
A BEAUTY from the inside to the out —
The angels are her sisters there's no doubt!!

I'm sure God swiped some blue right from the skies —
And placed it in the color of her eyes!
Set loose some rays of sunshine for her hair —
And destined life-long YOUTH for her to wear!!

He pondered and He searched a long, long while —
For just the PERFECT quality of smile!
And fashioned it in such a timeless way —
That still it's smiling bright, even today!!

Her tears are like the early morning dew —
Like droplets on the rose's radiant hue.
(Emotions do not always come with reason —
He gave them to us like the changing season.)

He portioned every joyful sound in half —
To formulate her very SPECIAL laugh.
And when He realized what He had made —
He placed her with her children, WHERE SHE
STAYED!!

And then to demonstrate she was the BEST —
He chose to make her taller than the rest!
(That's not to say they're aren't others too —
But who compares to her? — A chosen few!!)

To teach in simply meant – to light the way –
Like sunlight separates the night from day.
But few will dare to share what's in the HEART –
It's THIS that sets the LADY so apart!

*And may I add this in 2009 –
MRS. GRADY keeps improving – just like WINE!
The BEST of TEACHERS keeps on getting BETTER –
AND BLESSED ARE THE CHILDREN WHO WILL
GET HER!!!

With Love, Gratitude and Continued Admiration!

1987 (*and 2009!)

Hail to the Chief – Of Washington School!!

For 53 years you've gone to school —
mostly in Bergenfield
As student and teacher and Principal —
But now it is time to yield.

You fought the good fight — did everything right —
living up to the standards you set
The greatest achievement in life is —
to never look back with regret

You utilized all of your talents —
making the most of your time
Always appearing Your Best —
so Handsome and Still in Your Prime!!

But time marches on for us —
What a Wonderful Tribute to say
How Wisely you chose to spend yours —
in Leadership — showing the way!

How many kids you have influenced! —
How many lives you have touched!
Setting a Steadfast Example —
Reflecting the Values you clutched.

To exercise such authority —
with the Utmost Respect as you do
Consistently standing your ground —
Yet a Gentleman through and through.

Maintaining this Marvelous Balance —
is a Strength Most Commendable!
Along with your other Fine Qualities —
like Kind – Supportive – Dependable!!

(Not to mention some obvious traits —
like being Well-Dressed for Success!
Those Fabulous Ties! The Spark in Your Eyes!
And Hair that has Never-Been-Messed!!)

You really made Quite an Impression —
on Faculty, Students and Staff!
With Strictly Professional Conduct —
Yet ready to share a good laugh!!!

Singing your praises is easy! –
No searching for rhymes or for reasons!
Summing it up is quite simple —
You're Truly A Man For All Seasons!!!!!

God Bless You Always Our Dear Mr. Wortche!!!!

With Love,
Kathie Rizzo and Faculty and Friends – June 2008

Farewell Song to Mr. Wortche
(to the tune of 'MacNamara's Band')

Oh his name is Mr. Wortche
he's the leader of our school
He's punctual and prudent
and he follows every rule

He loves to tell a story
and he wears the greatest ties
If Kuchar gave out trophies –
he would surely win the prize!

Oh Nancy Glen and Rocco
and the faculty agree –
A credit to old Bergenfield –
is Principal Hen-ry!

Oh his name is Mr. Wortche
he's the leader of us all
He wears a well-trimmed mustache
and he's also very tall

His suits are very tailored
and his hair is always neat
He is the finest principal
that you will ever meet!

Oh the school bells ring – the students sing –
and Mendelsohn will play
A credit to old Bergenfield
is our own Hen-ry!

Oh his name is Mr. Wortche
he's the leader we admire
And though he is the greatest –
now he's ready to retire!

His service in this school will be
a real hard thing to match
Whoever gets him next –
is surely getting quite a catch!

Oh his smile is dear – his style sincere –
And his family's something grand
A credit to old Bergenfield is Henry – he's the man!!!!
A credit to old Bergenfield –––– is Henry –
he's the man!!!!!!!!!!

Upon Your Retirement

Working with you
Has been very nice
As we bid you farewell
May we give this advice –
Take time to do
The things that you like
Just try not to fall
Off of your motorbike!
For you're no 'Spring Chicken'
Even though you might think
(Joan tells us you even wobble
On your skates at the rink!)

Throw out your alarm clock
And turn up the T.V.
You'll want to stay up now
To see what's to see
Watch Leno and Conan
Or Dave Letter-man
You've just joined the Club
Of Late Night T.V. Fan
Then stay in your jammies
It's O.K. to sleep late
Don't bother to shave now
Those whiskers can wait!

For Ellen DeGeneres
Comes on at ten
You can dance right along
Like you did way back when
(Just make sure the shades

Are pulled down real tight –
You wouldn't want the neighbors
To capture this sight!)
But should you oversleep
And miss out on this heaven
Jerry Springer and The View
Both come on at eleven!!

To The Carlstadt Retired Teachers – With Love

Retirement is proof that dreams can come true
At the end of an awesome career.
Countless rewards are in store for you –
A time to slow down and be freer!

Some of you planned your retirement –
For some it's a hard pill to swallow.
In spite of emotions and sentiments
You'll sure be a tough act to follow!

The excellent standards you set –
The leadership that you portrayed –
As role models we'll never forget –
And on Tuesdays together you prayed!

To ensure that they didn't ignore you –
You found ways to keep kids inspired!
No wonder your students adore you –
And by parents you're so admired!

You'll never know the changes you brought –
How you influenced a brand new direction!
Heart and soul in the lessons you taught –
With calm and consistent affection!

Went above and beyond for the school –
So rejoice and enjoy your new station!
It's time for some rest and renewal –
With some well deserved relaxation!

I stole this line from a teacher mug –
For I'm really not all that clever –
With every star and sticker and hug –
You "Teachers touch lives forever!"

God bless you all now as you leave here –
You raised the bar on a job well done!
And exceeded it year after year!
The impressions you made will live on!!!

06–24–10

Pat's Farewell

No more pencils – no mare books –
No more students' puzzled looks!
No more Conferences 'til ten –
Then getting up next day again!!

No report cards – no more grades –
No more Halloween parades!
No more bells to make you nervous –
No more Workshops and "In-Service!!"

No more Budgets – no more PIPS –
Or counting money for Class Trips!
Done with hearing tattle-tales –
Done with Bergenfield Web-Mails!!

No more commutes in the rain –
Or early telephone Snow Chain!
No Observations – or Book Fairs –
Or eating lunch on little chairs!!

"Partial Sums" can take a hike –
"Frames and Arrows" – and the like!
Throw away your last red pen –
Never write in red again!!

Terra Nova – kiss good-bye –
(Don't it make ya wanna cry?)
Good-bye book bags – Manuals too –
Lesson Plans – no longer due!!

Files and Folders – disappear!
End of school is finally here!!
Take your apron off the hook –
Time to garden – Time to cook!!!

Sleep through breakfast – go for brunch!
Take a nap – then go for lunch!!
No more papers left to mark –
So take the baby to the park!!!

Through with blackboards – through with chalk –
Read a book – or take a walk!
Then rest again so you won't tire –
You'll be wide-awake for Choir!!

Delete your e-mail – Shut it down!
Spend an evening on the town!!
Committee meetings now are through
Take some time for Pete and You!!

(Rumor has it – long ago –
The Convent called you – yes or no?
Heads or Tails – you'd be a nun –
The coin was flipped – 'Twas Pete that won!
Then Pat and Pete went on a date –
And after – went from 'Good to Great'!!
Here's proof they made the perfect choice –
Two Fine careers – and Two Fine Boys!!!)

In Bergenfield – with years well served –
Retired Bliss – is well deserved!
So make a toast – and pour the vino!
God Bless You Always – Pat Monchino!!!!!!!

For Michael

We are the Class of '66
We grew and changed and stayed the same
The world will shine a little brighter
We lit a corner with our flame.

We're in the songs the Beatles wrote
Survived the nuns – and Vietnam
We laughed and cried before each other
And shared the dance floor at the prom.

Years and distance can't unbind us
Separation is only miles
The bond is unintimidated
By success – and failures – and lifestyles.

So rare a love like ours exists
So timeless is the joy we share
A love that can't divorce or kill us
What other love could prove so fair?

There is a power shining o'er us
That like the moon effects the sea
Perpetuating waves of love
Connecting us eternally

Don't you leave before I see you
Don't you go before I come
Remember – I'm a part of you
We're whole and equal by our sum.

We are the class of '66
We really cannot get much higher
We have it all right now you know
We're God – and family – you and I are.

(Michael Conlon)

1989

I'm a Teacher

I am a teacher you see
My hours are eight until three
I have to dress neat –
Stand all day on my feet –
And I love every child I see.

I'll never get rich on my pay
Still I keep coming back every day
I am hardly a saint –
I just love finger paint –
Traded wealth just to watch children play.

There are times when I ask why I do it
Wonder if there is any sense to it
Though it's sometimes obscure –
Of one thing I am sure –
I'm a teacher and I always knew it!

The pros and the cons I've been weighing
My failures and doubts keep me praying
But there's a light that I see –
Might be coming from me –
And as long as I see it – I'm staying!

I guess you could say that I love it
In spite of the stress that comes of it
The kids are a test
But they bring out my best
Even teach me to rise up above it!

Hugs and kisses keep coming my way
I get valentines nearly each day
Where else could I go
To be treated just so
Where the fringe benefits outweigh the pay!

A job with adults leaves me cold
With the children I'd rather grow old
For each day I'm renewed
Though at times I'm unglued!
The reward – is more precious than gold.

4. SUMMER

Summer Love
(4 Kids and 19 Years Later!)

Remember my love, how you loved me
The summer before we were wed?
How we spoke of our dreams and our visions
And the sand on the beach was our bed.

Remember the lake where we swam
And the breeze in the trees and the sun?
And the way that we looked at each other?
The world was all ours, just for fun.

Today I went back to that place
And brought with me our little boy.
Our dreams and our visions are ours to behold –
And the world is all his, just for joy!

And I remembered the way that you loved me,
The summer before we were wed.
And it wasn't as sweet as the love that we shared
This morning right here in our bed.

Birdsense

How I love my Summer walks
In evenings when it's cool
My limbs all loose and limber
From a visit to the pool.

With crickets in the background
My thoughts reverberate
The list of Summer things to do
Before it gets too late.

Too late! Too late! To late – for what?
I heard a night-bird call
What does not get accomplished now –
Can simply wait 'til Fall!

To set the Summer list aside
Is such a Big Relief!
No wonder that the weeks fly by
And Summer seems so brief!!

What a brilliant notion!
Deadlines are absurd!!
Stressing's such a waste of time
I heard it from – a bird!!

I do so love those evening walks
Perspective I regain
To communicate with nature
Is to stabilize my brain!!

Summer Nights

The air is hot and heavy
I cannot walk too fast
The crickets' steady chirping
Signing off the day that's past.

Nocturnal Summer music
The air-conditioners' hum
Cars and planes and train sounds
Of travelers to and from.

The buzz of a mosquito
Cicadas in the trees
The spider spins in silence
Summer nights are all of these.

July 2005

The Good Night Kiss

On June 14th a Firefly
Blinked at me as I walked by
A Catbird in a nearby tree
Caught my eye and greeted me.

In sandaled feet and sleeveless arms
I am seduced by Summer's charms
To walk the streets in after hours
Soothing thoughts the soul empowers.

Whispering breezes that convey
Assessment of the ending day
Nature's good night kiss it seems
A perfect prelude for my dreams.

Cricket Talk

Beneath the light of a cloudy moon
The very first cricket on the 12th of June
Told me that Summer was on its way
How pleasant a thought at the end of my day!

It made me sigh behind my smile
To think how Spring – only lasts a while
I breathed in deeply the changing air
Exhaling freely my every care!

I'm lighter than before my walk
All due to the tune of – Cricket Talk!
I'm born again when the crickets sing
Anticipating what Summer will bring.

Can an insect really be the reason –
For the change in me at the change of the season?
Remember the story from long ago –
'Twas a cricket that saved Pinocchio!

06–12–06

Camper's Farewell

I really can't believe –
it's almost time to leave
The days have flown so fast –
I hoped they'd last and last
I know it's time to go –
'Cuz my socks are smellin' so!
My money is all spent –
and there's a chipmunk in my tent!
I really love to hike –
but I miss my ten-speed bike!
I lost my father's flashlight –
I've got the BIGGEST BUGBITE!!
Glen Spey has so much charm –
the lake is nice and warm
The rocks have beauty too –
unless one's in your shoe!
I especially love the trees –
(I could do without the bees)!
The deer played hide and seek –
my sneakers sprang a leak!
The counselors are the Best –
They put us to the test
They made us swim and float –
I even rowed the boat!
They also made us clean –
With brooms we were a team!
Beppie made us sing –
and bandaged everything –
D.J.'s Mr. Fixit –
and Tom knows how to mix it!
With Lisa as our leader –
The staff lounge will be neater!

The tubers had to follow –
or the Delaware would swallow!
If not for Wendy and Mare –
I'd still be floating there!
The campers were entranced –
when the counselors even danced!
The kids, you had to see –
Eat your heart out MTV!!
If I hear one more 'Dead Cow'
I will hitchhike home right now!
A few words on behalf
of our European Staff
We hope you love Glen Spey –
and come back again someday
For it always will be here –
So let's meet again next year!

1987

Summer's Exit

Sweet Summer song
Serenade my soul!
I sense a subtle shifting
Of the season into Fall.

The wisdom of the crickets
Is muffled in the night
A flock of birds just up and left –
A melancholy sight.

A pair of pensive robins
Hopped within my view
As I looked out my window
And then away they flew!

Robins on the lawn
Are quite the usual thing
Except the message they conveyed
Was – 'See you in the Spring!'

I observed in reverent pause
Like the changing of the guard
Transition of the seasons
Right before me in my yard.

Cooler are the evenings now
It's chilly in the morn.
Just today I threw away
My sandals over-worn.

Apples are abundant
Sweet corn is getting scarce
To Summer's ripe tomatoes –
Nothing quite compares.

Autumn whispers softly
At first we don't believe
Fall's ambiguous entrance –
As Summer takes its leave.

09-23-06

Summerfall

The day was almost over
As I started on my walk
Barking dogs heard in the distance
'Neath the bushes – Cricket talk.

Children's laughter from their backyards
Dusk descending like a sigh
Humid breezes kiss the treetops
Before the Summer green leaves die.

The changing of the seasons
Fills my senses with a rush
Flowers dried up but still standing
In a quiet, solemn hush –

In tribute to the garden
That was almost Paradise
Near the pool that's now been covered
To protect from snow and ice!

There should be a name for seasons –
For the seasons in-between
Before the leaves are golden
But no longer really green.

Neither Summer now nor Autumn
(Earthen puberty it seems!)
Memories of ocean sunsets
Left to hover in my dreams.

5. FAITH

A Prayer for Hope and Change in 2009

Heavenly Father, forgive me –
for weakness, intolerance and fear
Though I agonize searching for answers –
solutions are not always clear.

I am who I am as You made me –
just trying to be my Best Self
At times, tangled up in emotions –
at the cost of my own mental health!

What can I do to make Changes? –
Help me to focus and see!
It's not about changing my family –
It's more about changes in me!!

I've walked in these old shoes so long –
I need to break in a new pair
Help me to stretch them to fit –
this new attitude that I wear!

I struggle to sort out the pieces –
to salvage the Love that survived
'To everything there is a season' –
and for me that day has arrived!

Please let me know that You're with me! –
I know I can't go it alone
I'm building my Hopes for Tomorrow –
on Today, with the seeds that I've sown.

My Prayer/Walk During Covid

My daily walk is such a gift –
to give my joints and spirit a lift!
With every step I contemplate –
not dwelling on what might be fate.
I seize the day the sun enhances –
it's spring! In spite of circumstances.
I meditate while birds are singing –
in awe am I, that spring keeps springing!

The season rules and still suffices –
the great outdoors all through the crisis –
With yellow dandelion dots –
and violets and forget-me-nots –
Bunnies in the yard are hopping –
and tulips in the garden popping!
Children in the sunshine happy –
and dressy daffodils so snappy!!

Sidewalk art with colored chalking –
makes me smile while I'm out walking.
Evidence of kids at play –
on this lovely sunny day!
Right on schedule the red-red robin –
in the yard is bob-bob-bobbin!
Blossoms on the trees are blooming –
bees are buzzing! Life's resuming!!

The air is cool – a soft wind blows –
a fragrant hyacinth fills my nose!
With this in mind my faith is stirred –
by scented flowers and calling bird.

My spirit's kindled through my senses –
I lift my heart and prayer commences –
"Oh heavenly father and mother who –
oversees the earth and its people too –
I beg your mercy and ask you please –
enlighten the cure for this awful disease!
Pour down your grace and your inspiration –
to scientists and researchers from every nation!
Unite us in this global war –
our faith in your healing power restore!
Protect and guide, I humbly beseech –
the healthcare workers whose hands outreach –
The living saints who risk their lives –
with hope that each of us survives!"

My walk is over – I return back home –
where here I sit to write this poem –
It's what I do in helpless times –
along with prayer – I turn to rhymes!
It lifts me up when I am down –
when friends and family aren't around.
My needy self ends with this prayer –
staying connected with you, I share.
I pray for us all in the end –
for each in my family and every friend –
"Give us this day for me and you –
our daily bread – and toilet paper too!
Amen." :)

My Prayer

I went to Sunday Mass today
And prayed with all my heart
For strength for friends and family
In the coming weeks to start.

I asked Our Heavenly Father
To comfort those in need
For courage for the living
And the suffering to be freed.

With eyes closed tight – and head bowed low
I knelt in solemn prayer
And named the folks in need of grace
And asked Him to be there.

Tonight I'll pray the Rosary
And contemplate each bead
Imploring Her to help us all
"Oh Mary – intercede."

I wish there was a way for me
To take away each sorrow
Instead – I'll leave it in His Hands –
And pray again tomorrow.

My Rosary

In the night I take up my beads
Make the Sign of the Cross and begin
Mother Mary – Bring Peace to the world
And help us to overcome sin.

As I finger each bead and recite
An umbrella of Hail Marys takes form
Over the heads of those I include
To protect them from life's every storm.

For my husband – to keep him on track
For my children – to protect and to guide
For my family and friends who are hurting
Let not their needs be denied.

Mother Mary – my own heart is aching
For nightmares I cannot control
Come close – Let me feel you beside me
Comfort – Enlighten – Console.

May no harm come to my children
And let not my children do harm!
Help me convey this sincerely to them
Without causing fret or alarm.

Soften the hearts of all leaders
Worldwide – Let all fighting cease!
Make all of our goals and endeavors
Collectively build a New Peace.

Give direction to all of our efforts
That we constantly follow His Way
Inspire us all – to do the right thing
In our actions by night and by day.

Let your Motherly Love rain upon those
Who are lost – or ill – or alone
Help me to serve others also
For my own horrid sins to atone.

As a wife and a mother and teacher
Open my eyes to Their needs
I know I can count on your presence
Each time that I reach for my beads.

09–14–03

For Mira – From Nonna and Nonno

Beautiful Mira
with the big brown eyes –
A gift from heaven –
a miraculous surprise!
Effervescent and pure
is the joy she can bring –
With a face new and lovely
as flowers in spring!

Her sweet voice and antics,
her smile and expressions
Every minute, every day –
makes us all count our blessings!
Living proof of God's power
and heavenly grace –
A sign of His love
sent for us to embrace!

The effect and impact
have uplifted our mood –
Bringing hope and faith
in our family renewed!
To Our Father
Who art in heaven we pray –
On this journey through parenthood –
please light the way!

Grant us the spirit,
the wisdom and strength –
In our efforts to guide her
through childhood – full length!
As instruments of unconditional
love and peace –
Through Mira You've given
our lives a new lease!

"And a child shall lead them."
We've heard that before
But our minds only dreamed
of what God had in store!
Our hearts sing Your praise
in our everyday living –
In grateful humility –
we extend our thanksgiving!

A Conversation with God

The unborn baby asked God his Father,
one day before his birth was near,
"How will I survive there on earth –
I'm so small and helpless; I fear –
I'm surrounded by love here in heaven –
where I can sing, dance and smile and laugh!"

Then God reassured that He had entrusted,
"A SPECIAL ANGEL IN YOUR BEHALF!
THIS SPECIAL ANGEL WILL NURTURE YOU -
THROUGH SONGS AND DANCE AND LAUGHTER
AND FILL YOUR LIFE WITH LOVE
AND ABUNDANCE –
LEAD YOU BACK TO ME HERE EVER AFTER.
SHE'S COUNTING THE MOMENTS FOR YOUR
COMING! –
PREPARING FOR YOUR EVERY NEED!
YOU'LL BE SURROUNDED WITH SUCH LOVE ON
EARTH! –
YOU'LL BE VERY HAPPY INDEED!!"

"But I don't even know the language! How will I ever
understand?"

"YOUR ANGEL'S WORDS ARE SWEET
AND LOVELY –
YOU'LL LEARN FROM HER AS I'VE PLANNED.
SHE'LL TEACH YOU ALL YOU NEED TO KNOW –
AND INSPIRE A LOVE OF LEARNING!
YOU ARE MY ANSWER TO HER PRAYERS –
THE WELL-DESERVED GIFT SHE'S BEEN
YEARNING."

"But how will I talk to You when I want – Will my angel show me the way?"

"YES! SHE'LL PLACE YOUR TWO HANDS TOGETHER –
WHEN SHE TEACHES YOU HOW TO PRAY."

"But who will protect me from harm – and keep me from getting lost?"

"YOUR ANGEL WILL RISK HER OWN LIFE FOR YOU – AND SACRIFICE NO MATTER THE COST!"

"But I will be sad not to see You. I'll miss Your presence in my new life."

"OH, I WILL ALWAYS BE PRESENT, MY CHILD –
IN YOUR JOY AND IN HARDSHIP AND STRIFE!
AND YOUR ANGEL WILL TELL YOU ABOUT ME –
SHE'LL NURTURE YOU SPIRITUALLY –
SHE'LL REMIND YOU THAT I'M ALWAYS NEAR YOU –
AND TEACH YOU THE WAY BACK TO ME."

Just then came the Heavenly moment –
With noise and excitement below!

"God, if I am to leave now please tell me –
For this angel I don't even know!
Who is she and what is her name? –
Then God responded with calm –
"LISTEN MY CHILD AND I'LL TELL YOU –
HER NAME IS QUITE SIMPLE – IT'S MOM."

I Believe

I believe in love and laughter –
Beauty in the world around
Here and now and then hereafter –
Joyful purposes abound!

Marching forth I mostly try –
Leading with my heart and hoping
Not to smother under "why?" –
Always leaving windows open.

Love keeps spreading like a garden –
Even in the coldest season
Though I ask to beg my pardon –
Love's forgiveness needs no reason.

Love and laughter as I'm working –
Love and laughter when I play
Negativity always lurking –
Bent on stealing joy away.

Times it latches on my ankle –
Pulls me down, entangles me
Faith and family leaves me thankful –
Treasured friendships set me free.

I believe that love is power –
Full of possibilities
Every season, every hour –
Opportunities to seize!

Remember daily if we could –
That mighty oak trees standing tall
Began beneath the Winter woods –
From little acorns in the Fall!

Imagination holds potential –
Inspirations come alive!
Anticipation is essential –
Believe – and watch them grow and thrive!!

Love and family, faith and friends –
Fields and forests filled with trees
The Spirit of God that never ends! –
I believe in all of these.

10-23-09

Last Morning (To the Sun)

Glow perfection on the world
      Your glare
Illusion tricks man's pride
      In belief the world would dare
      To meet you eye to eye.

But I in all humility
      (Tho humble not be me)
      Am not so blinded in your blinding stare
      Unable yet to see
         The truth you blind us with.

Forgive my nonsense controversy
      (As some would think it so)
      I am nationless
      But know my place in lost identity
      And do accept your golden scourge
      And know full well what for.

Forgive observance
      Clearly overlooking truth
      So clear and clearly in its source
      (I don't pretend of course to understand.)

Some sort of self-preservent game
      They play with time
      Convenient come the words
      In temporary cure but I'm
      So small and dare not play –
      Or quit.

Ignorant and weak but wise in this
      Your truth in blinding splendored light
      Yields brilliance, dazzling strength
      To face the night
      That follows all last mornings.

And better blind we are
      Deny the horror from our eyes!
      And shield the pompous self who sees and dies
      Those "thousand deaths."

And blind me! Blind me in the morning from all truth
      Except your glorious light
      To guide my weary footsteps
      In the long and lonely night –
      That follows all last mornings.

Does selfishness make fat the self that longs
      Or do I further dare imply
      My lonely self in want for warmth – along with
      light?
      And did I not already humbly state – my being
      weak?

Or will your fire
      Enrapture all
         Including cold
            That's sure to follow this
               Last morning...

          Kathie Pell 1967

Ultimate Devotion

U ntil the
L ove of
T he Creator
I nspired your existence,
M usic belonged only to the
A ngels
T hat served to praise Him and His universe including
E arth which He gave us as our beautiful home.

D on't
E ver forget the
V alue
O f your unique
T alent — and use it wisely to
I nspire yourself and
O thers to draw
N earer to The Spirit.

With Love from
Your Biggest Fan

Despair

Who is this God
She speaks of
That twists
And turns
And tortures in the night
And chokes the cherries
In her cheeks
To white.
What hunger motivates
Him to
Devour the pure and precious pearl
And leave the shell to rot
Upon the sands of time?
Is this The Son
Whose hand once touched
And Healed
A million oozing sores
And mended mangled men
Bringing light to blinded eyes?
Is this The Christ
Whose presence penetrated peace?
Do His powers not persist
Beyond the flesh?
Or are we the 'children's children'
Women wept for
On His bitter bloody route to Calvary?
Did He only live
To show us how
To die?

Kathie Pell 1968

Help!

Jesus who once calmed the sea –
Put out Your Hand upon me.
I am tossing and losing my way,
Worried and frightened this day.

This journey is part of Your Plan –
I can only succeed by Your Hand.
Please spend some time in my boat,
Your presence will keep me afloat.

Amen

Night Lights

Like a silent city in the sky
The shining stars above me where I lie
Each a tiny distant window lit
I strain my eyes in search to fathom it.

I feel the Holy Presence of the Power
Creator of the day, the night, the hour;
Illuminator of the dark of night –
I am humbled by infinity in light.

The sunset on the lake, the crickets song
The world's the church to which we all belong.
My children and the man I'm now part of
Are teachers in the rituals of love.

The constant celebration is all ours,
As many ways to worship as the stars.
The prayers we share in church upon our knees,
Or in our hearts beneath the stars and trees.

Glen Spey
Aug. 1987

6. GUIDANCE

Mom's ABCs For Living a Good and Happy and Healthy Life

Anger makes a messy spill!
Anger managed – is a useful skill!

Be kind! Make up your mind! –
To everyone – every time!

Care for the earth! She is your mother! –
Care for yourself – and one another!

Do unto others and help those in need.
You'll be blessed 10 times over – for every good deed!

Exercise daily – your body and mind! –
Exhale and leave useless worries behind!

Friends are like flowers in the garden of life!
Find some – and be one, in good times and strife!

God is Love and the Source of all Good! –
Seek Grace and Guidance to live as you should!

Help where you can – in big ways or small!
Lending a hand – costs nothing at all!

Invest in the children and give them your time! –
Be a positive influence while they're young, in their
prime!

Joy is contagious! So spread some around! –
Hold your head up high! – Keep your feet on the
ground!

Kindle your love-light and let it shine! –
Let love light the way and all will be fine!

Live every day like it is your last! –
Treasure each moment – for life moves so fast!

Make the most of your talents, whatever they are! –
Sparkle! For you are a Shining Star!!

Never hold grudges! – Forgive and forget! –
This is by far – the best advice yet!!

Overlook the small stuff! – Keep a healthy
perspective! –
When choosing your battles – be very selective!

Pray! And believe in the Power of Prayer! –
Every day – every night – any time – any where!!

Quiet your mind! – Take time to relax,
to keep you from getting all stressed to the max!

Remember the good times! – Release all the bad! –
Talk about the Best Times in life that you've had!

Sing! Sing a song! –
Make it Simple to last your whole life long!

Tune out all negativity! –
Tune in to positivity!!

Use the gifts that God has given –
to guide you in your path – faith-driven!

Value the lessons that you have learned! –
And Value the blessings in life you have earned!

Wear your smile! – And not just for show!! –
It's a powerful mood changer – more than you know!

Xpress your love in big ways and small! –
And don't hold back! – You've got plenty for all!!

You have a purpose here on God's earth! –
Follow His Love-Light – And you will find worth!

Z's are important! Make sure you get yours! –
(Earplugs are helpful – if somebody snores!!)

Comp–Heart–Ments

Find me a shelf for my feelings
Give me a drawer for my heart
Make room in a closet
To store my emotions
When they loosen and fall apart

Have you a vase for my teardrops?
One that's deep and dark – to conceal
And set in a basin
I can depend on
That won't overflow when I feel.

A bureau might be appropriate!
My sorrows I'll place in each drawer
In back are reserved my regrets;
In the front, my doubts I will store.

Each little sadness I'll fold up
Each lonely night without sleep
I know I could tidy my life up –
With a place for each feeling to keep.

I need a container for anger and stress –
Preferably one with a lid on!
And a corner where I can always be sure –
That they will stay perfectly hidden!

I know when these moods come to surface,
They really create quite a pressure!
Perhaps in my hamper I'll toss them next time!
Or maybe a chest or my dresser!!

God put me together completely;
And packaged my feelings there too
But I just don't know where I should keep them –
So please tell me! What do You do???????

1988

Changes

Spring and Summer – Fall and Winter –
the seasons come and go.
In timeless repetition –
that still surprises even though.

Miraculous performance
of Mother Nature's mission –
Beauty overlapping –
overcomes in smooth transition.

Fluctuating temperatures
give way to sudden change –
And redecorate the landscape –
as colors rearrange.

Daylight Savings Time reflects
an introspective shift –
An ordinary sunset –
Is an extraordinary gift!

It's hard to name the colors
in the painted sky above –
Intense and interchanging –
so very much like love!

In splendid pinks and golden hues
the setting sun enlightens –
With every breath – as I review –
my own awareness heightens!

Inevitable the Winter comes –
as daylight becomes less –
A wave of immortality
invades my consciousness.

Spring and Summer – Fall and Winter –
the seasons by and by –
Our spiritual evolution – Life –
between the earth and sky.

Advice For Newlyweds

Now that your wedding is nearing –
Lots of advice you'll be hearing
There's plenty of wisdom in store –
And lots of 'old wives tales' galore!

Advice filled with all good intentions –
And the counseling's free not to mention!
The 'helpful hints' list never ends –
From well-meaning family and friends.

I'm an old family friend and so hence –
Allow me to add my two cents!
Married 40 years now (and it shows!) –
I've got lots to say, so here goes!!

There are circumstances that you will scorn –
And issues that can leave you torn
To "be right" or "be kind," you must choose –
Go for "kind," and you'll never lose.

Try not to hurt one another –
(Nurture Love or Love's fire will smother!)
But remember, at times if you do –
Say you're sorry and don't let it stew.

Doesn't matter who is to blame –
Holding grudges is such a bad game
Hurting still comes down to this –
A boo-boo heals best with a kiss!

Before criticizing, Think Twice –
You get what you give, so Be Nice!
(But remember we humans are weak –
So know when to turn the other cheek!)

Don't be fussy or petty or picky –
Accepting each other is Tricky!
This advice you won't find in a book –
Overlook – Overlook – Overlook!!!

Make sure when you turn out the light –
Any wrongs of the day are made right
You won't always see eye to eye –
But to keep Love Alive – YOU MUST TRY!!

KEEP ON TRYING – and don't be a quitter! –
(Especially if little feet patter-pitter!)
A Good Marriage takes PATIENCE and TIME –
(It's not always easy to rhyme!!)

Work like a couple of dogs! –
Sleep well, like a couple of logs!!
Eat and drink and be merry! –
How happy should you two be? VERY!!

Try not to "sweat the small stuff" –
PRAY, when the going gets tough!
No matter the mood you are in –
Laughter's the Best Medicine!!!!!

THE SECRET TO HAPPINESS IN LIFE –
Is the key to overcoming strife
So develop it later or sooner –
A SHORT MEMORY – AND A GREAT SENSE OF
HUMOR!!!!!!!!!!!!!!!

02–02–08

To the "King of My World"
(With Love from Your Queen)

I fell in love with a gentleman –
For his passionate eyes and his heart –
For his way with the children –
He's one in a million! –
Sensible – handsome – and smart!!

You are still that handsome gentleman, Paul –
You are all that I knew you would be –
You stayed by my side –
Raised our family with pride –
You're the king of my world to me!

Now at a fork in the road you stand –
Setting your sights on a goal –
I gave you my blessing –
Without second guessing –
Your competency in that role.

But I've never been much for politics –
The truth and the facts are confusing –
It boggles my brain –
On my humor puts a strain –
I prefer to seek out what's amusing.

I don't have command of the lingo –
Or the savvy to play in the game –
To support you I'll try –
But I won't fake or lie –
Not for title – position – or fame.

For alas you are king of my world!
And henceforth – I am your queen!
While you sit on your throne –
I've got one of my own –
Don't let politics come in between!!

I pray that my wonderful gentleman –
By his ego is not overcome –
That he'll just put aside –
All arrogance and pride –
With his mind and his heart he should run!

Somewhere there's a quote in The Bible –
That hits the nail right on the head!
What will you gain –
In the end if you trade –
My respect for a title instead?!

So please remain close beside me –
Keeping your feet on the ground –
Come what may in November –
Please always remember –
Long ago in my heart you were crowned!

I fell in love with a gentleman!
Forty some odd years ago –
For his passionate eyes –
And his ways that were wise –
And that's the man I still know!!!

And keep it that way! – Kath

05–18–11

185

Old – But Not Cold

What can be said about growing old
That hasn't already been said?
For starters – we know it's best not to complain –
Since the only alternative – is DEAD!!

From the mirrors we run – but we never can hide
Try not too close to observe
New spots and wrinkles turn up every day
There's a bulge – where there once was a curve!

Bones are protruding right next to my toes
And my legs are all blotchy and blue!
I have to lie down now – to put on my hose –
It's a sight – but what else can I do?

Push-ups and Cover-ups and Criss-Cross Support
Girdles, Orthotics and such
All sorts of efforts to keep things in place –
But contraptions can just do so much!!

Eye creams and Cold creams and Never-Grow-Old
creams
And creams that reduce cellulite!
All covered in lotion – I just got the notion –
I might slip off my bed in the night!!!!!

My gums keep receding – Bifocals I'm needing
Keeping up with my roots is a chore!
Good thing that Carson retired when he did –
'Cuz I can't stay up late anymore!!

Remembering "stuff" has become a real challenge
Like appointments – a number – a name
Brain cells are turning to oatmeal it seems!
To "Senior Moments" – we attribute the blame!!

Still – I'll pass on procedures like Botox
I'll just let Mother Nature take care
My husband still tells me I'm pretty
And I love him Much More – without hair!!!!

The Little Garden

My neighbor's little garden
is a source of conversation
She tends and tidies, trims and grooms
with patient dedication
The garden sits between two stoops –
a modest three by seven –
Hardly worth the effort you'd think –
but a little patch of heaven!

In Spring her daffodils perform
and sway in perfect line –
The radiant roses sing her praises –
come the Summertime!
Assorted mums and flowers of Fall
are vibrantly displayed –
Burgundy, gold and orange –
show off Autumn on parade!

Yet in the background roses
thrive and loyally remain
The secret of their heartiness –
we simply can't explain!
The roses not to be upstaged,
headline – the main attraction –
They bloom and flaunt their robust beauty –
and gloat with satisfaction!

In December when trees are bare
and Autumn leaves have dried –
My neighbor's roses maintain their stance
with elegance and pride!
As days grow short and bitter cold –
we marvel at the sight –
Delicate but sturdy roses –
in brilliance bloom – still upright!

In mid-December we photographed
the rose in grand display –
In that tiny little garden –
a miracle on Christmas Day!
Precious is the power
of this awesome daily pleasure –
My neighbor's little garden
may be small but it's a treasure!!

April 2016

Congratulations Natalie!

Natalie – you made it through four grueling years!
Overcame the obstacles with laughter, and tears!!
The journey continues – with you at your best!
To face every challenge and ace every test!!

Your future looks bright – you have made some good
choices!
Seek sound advice – and follow those voices!!
Words of wisdom as your goal you approach –
From your kindergarten teacher – and old swimming
coach!!

To thine own self be true – to your family show love –
Pray often to Our Father – in heaven above!
Hold onto your dreams – but remember this fact –
Life at its best – is a balancing act!

It's a big buffet – but you can't have it all!
The best gifts you have – didn't come from a mall!!
When everything seems like it's way too much –
Find comfort in friendship and your family's touch.

You're the best you can be – at the top of your game!
Closing in on the prize you're preparing to claim!
Focus in on your dreams – with eyes open wide –
Determine the pace – but take it in stride!!

Again I remind you – at the end of the day –
To quiet your mind – lift your heart up and pray –
Just a glimmer of faith is all you will need –
Not bigger than the proverbial 'mustard seed!'

Hold on to it tight – and don't ever let go!
I'm giving you this – so you'll always know –
You've been blessed with your life in so many ways –
Count these blessings when you're having bad
days!!.........

You are talented! Creative!! A dancer and singer!!
A researcher, author and – synchronized swimmer!!!
You've sure made the most of the gifts you received –
Way back in kindergarten – who would have
believed??!!!!

You have faith – and family –
and friendship – and health!!
You have beauty – you're brainy –
it all counts as wealth!!!
You're such a hard worker –
and with so much to give –
People will love you for
as long as you live!!!!!!!!!!!!!!!!!!!!!

05–31–08

To Luke and Carley as You Graduate

I can't believe so soon you're moving on! –
the years have flown so very fast!
Way too quickly childhood has come and gone! –
our hopes and expectations you've surpassed!
As a Christian man and woman – comes the test –
the challenges you'll face still lie ahead.
With precious family love you have been blessed! –
now follow in the path that Jesus led!
Find a need and fill it – best you can –
when others take the low road – you go high!
Money and fine things don't make the man! –
the best in life – money still can't buy!
Our faith & love & charity –
marks us in the end –
'the greatest bring love' – said he –
for enemy and friend!
Now that message can prove really tough! –
but with God's grace you'll manage!
When you find that life gets rough –
trust in faith as your advantage!
Tears and fears are part of life –
don't be ashamed to share!
Everyone has stress and strife –
reach out with love and prayer!
When given the choice to 'be right' or 'be kind' –
let Jesus be your light!
Sometimes we need to put ego behind –
being 'kind' is more godly – than 'right'!
Well there you have it dear young hearts! –
with love and with pride I convey!
In addition to having such good looks and smarts! –
may you grow in God's goodness I pray!

Always remember how special you are! –
even when things may go wrong –
Keep being you and shine like a star! –
Dance your dance and sing your own song!

In Silence

Affection integrates our flesh
        Ignites our souls
Breathing feeds the fire
All that is real touches
        In time
And nothing touches
That is not real.
              For reality is sensitive to time
              Like truth to love.

Silence!
But fools in contradiction
        Build highways next to parks
        Make typewriters talk in libraries
And intrude on solitude
        With obnoxious cries – for peace.

Silence?
"Breeds idleness and sin!"
In the eyes of worldly cynics
Who wallow in their words
        And smirk – and disapprove
And lovers are "naïve"
But
Love finds refuge in the night
        Seclusion in serenity
While the weak conform to sleep
        The shallow seem to die
            In silence –
            Where only love survives.

Kathie Pell 1968

To You, My Students, In 1992

You're Columbus in 1492 –
What in the World will you do?
What's going on in your mind?
What in your dreams do you find?

You're full of ideas – and so curious!
There are plenty who don't take you serious!
You are eager and burn with desire!!
There are those who would put out the fire!!

But enlightened by what you conceived,
You hold on to the truth you believe.
Isabel recognized your persistence –
For your courage, she granted assistance.

With so many – so sure – you would fail –
By the light of your faith, you set sail.
"You Can't Change the World!" cried the others.
But You Did – with the Truth you discovered!!

****

You are YOU in 1992.
What in the World will YOU do?
What's going on in YOUR mind??
What in Your Dreams do You find??

Are you thinking about world pollution?
With Knowledge – You'll find a solution.
What of Cancer, Leukemia and Aids?
Wear Your Courage – and don't be afraid!

With Faith – you can change things for sure.
Maybe YOU will discover the cure!!
Forget what the others might say –
Change the world in Your own special way.

There will always be those who'll conspire –
But don't let them put out Your fire!
There's no challenge that You cannot face –
With Courage – and Knowledge – and God's Grace!

Disregard what "they" say – Pay no heed.
Armed with Knowledge – and Faith – Take the Lead!!
Past the Horizon – Sail Free!
The Truth – lies beyond what you see.

Love Grows

Greatest Moment ever had –
Brand New Mother – Brand New Dad!
Purest Blossom set to bloom –
Little infant in the womb.

Courtship – Marriage – Parenthood –
Good things come from All Things Good!
Man and Woman – bound as one –
Love conceived – New Life begun!!

The Hand of God bestows His Grace –
His Masterpiece – This Precious Face!
Radiating Love's First Kiss –
Miracles are made from This!!!

In awe we study every feature –
And question how to be the teacher
Advice pours in from all around –
Hard to know which piece is sound!

Parenting is quite a test! –
In the end – You'll do Your Best!!
Think of what the garden needs –
As seedlings grow from tiny seeds –

Lots of sunlight – water – air –
Lots of Time and Lots of Care!
The Simple Truth – is one we know –
Nurture Love and watch Love Grow!!!

Feb. 2008

197

To the Women of the Years

I haven't come down from the clouds just yet
You've got me walking on air!
You gave me a night I'll never forget –
I still can't believe I was there!!

Is it possible I was dreaming?
I've been pinching myself ever since!
My husband so proud he's just beaming!
Now I'm following in his footprints!!

Contributing to the community
Is quite a big order to fill!
You gals do so much for humanity –
You're not just the "run of the mill"!!

But li'l ol' me – what do I do?
I just wish I was more deserving!
Fundraising to me is still new –
While year after year you've been serving!!!

YOU are the Women of the Years!
Every day and for so many reasons –
YOU have MY applause and my cheers!
YOU are truly – Women for all seasons!!!

YOU are the Movers and Shakers!
Running to meetings at night –
With raffles and other money makers –
While I swim and dance and write!!!

Your organization is Tops!
You're the women that I most admire!!
The Eveready Bunny never stops –
Doing good – never seeming to tire!!!

I am humbled to think I was chosen
I am honored to be in your midst!
From hearing my name – I'm still frozen –
Cuz I'm still not quite sure what I didst!!

Nevertheless – I accept!
Did I mention – I'm still on Cloud Nine??
Thanks to you I have hardly much slept –
Not believing this trophy is mine!!

I don't know quite how to say thanks –
If you'll have me – I'd sure like to stay!
Is there room for one more in the ranks??
 - Can't thank 'em – then join 'em – I say!!

Just say the word that I'm in –
I'll get going in two seconds flat!
Tell Paul that I'll be late for din –
I am out shopping for white gloves and a hat!!!

A.C.O.A.

How do I answer my children
When they ask why their grandparents don't visit?
Shall I tell them they're both alcoholic?
Not much of an answer now – is it?

Do I tell them how sick they both are?
But then what kind of daughter am I
Not to run to their sides to assist them
Don't I care if they live or they die?
Can I tell them I wish things were different?
Can I ever expect them to see?
That I had to jump off of the carousel
For what it was doing to me.

I'll describe all the times I was there for them
I really did try, I'll explain
I prayed and I tried – and I cried and I cried –
But my efforts and tears were in vain.

Dad just wouldn't give up his drinking
No matter what he put us all through
Mom resigned to abuse – lost her mind on the way
A victim of alcohol too.

But what can I say to my children
When their curious questions arise?
The truth puts a lump in my throat
Memories still bring tears to my eyes.

They don't know that I miss them so badly
For the years that they're wasting away
The caring and sharing that should have been ours
Is a loss that I suffer each day.

I wish they could look in my heart
And see how the distance evolved
The lies and the fighting, the heartaches and shame
Through the years, caused our love to dissolve.

'How come Grandma and Grandpa don't come here?'
'How come we never even go there?'
'How come you cry when you hang up the phone?'
'And why are their names in our prayer?'

I wanted to give you a childhood
That was happy and healthy and free
Surrounded with comfort and love
The way that a family should be.

I've worked very hard to achieve this
And there's nothing that I wouldn't do
I've had to accept the things I can't change –
When you grow up – I hope you will too.

1989

Night Frights!

When I was a child
I dreaded the night
The darkness surrounding
So filled me with fright

The stillness, the background
For each scary sound,
While headlights cast shadows
That made my heart pound!

Under the blanket
There wasn't much air
Suffocation seemed harmless
Compared to out there!

Ghosts and Gorillas
Just waiting to snatch
At my throat, if I so much as
Opened my hatch!

Beasties and Boogey Men
Under my bed!
A Tiger in my closet
Ready to be fed!

Skeleton in the windows!
And Spooks on the drapes!!
Vampires and Witches
In shadowy capes!!!

"Let it be morning!" I'd pray,
"Let it come!"
'Til frozen and breathless
To sleep I'd succumb.

Relieved, I'd awaken
To daylight and then,
When night came
I hid 'neath my blankets again!

In spite of the "demons" –
I've flourished and grown
And now I'm a parent
With kids of my own.

Those "monsters" no longer
Come into my room
But the kids call on Me now
To come in and shoo 'em!

The mystery the night brings
Can poison the mind,
With gross encounters
Of the very worst kind!

And so in the night
When I'm called upon for
A creature who's hiding
Behind a closed door –

I pause and remember
And handle with care,
For not long ago
It was Me under there!!

Thought Therapy

Dip myself inside of me
I've got it all in there
Rely upon my memories
To heal me like a prayer.

Images of Mountains
Medication for the mind
Lovely Lakes and Soothing Rivers
Within me flow and wind.

I have only to remember
All the places I have been
Nature's Bounty, Scenic Beauty
Treasures here within.

Take time from stress and pressure
Close my eyes and contemplate
Whales are spouting off at Maui
Sunset on the Golden Gate.

Panoramic Riviera
Taste the Wine along the way
Cross the Peace Bridge into Canada
Feel the fine Niagara Spray!

Spend a second in the Alps
A minute in Agropoli
Blink my way to Puerto Rico
Sail upon her Turquoise Sea.

Gardened Grounds and Gracious Mansions
Farms on Hillsides, Cornfields groomed
Peaceful Deer along the roadside
Miles of Meadows where Wildflowers bloomed.

On the Bleakest Night of Winter
Recall the warmth of Sand and Sun
Reminisce among my Travels
Remember up a time of fun!

Every venture every journey
Leaves its imprint on the soul
Call upon its healing powers
Let it comfort and console.

1989

Mission Accomplished

M ore and more I'm thinking
      there's a reason we are here.

I t seems we have a purpose –
      though at times it's not so clear.

S ometimes moving forward –

S ometimes moving back –

I nteresting – the zig-zag path –

O bstacles on the track!

N ow and then awareness – reveals an inspiration

A ll at once a clarity – an internal revelation!

C hrissy took it by the reins – and followed in pursuit!

C onquering her darkest days – to her demons gave
      the boot!

O vercame addictions and went on to counsel others –
      thru W.W., Karate and Aerobics
      for the mothers!

M ostly you'd expect defeat by Cancer as a rule –
      She took surgery & chemo and completed
      Beauty School!

P leased her customers one-by-one —
      knowing well her fate and.

L oving up her family lots — before it was too late.

I nsisted Julie gather every bit of teenage joys —
      in spite of the inevitable —
      which they faced with strength and poise.

S ons are all too precious — and Chrissy's are no less —

H er Frankie, Mike and Julie
      by her spirit will be blessed!

E ver loyal Vinnie too, who steadfastly stood by —
      and Mother Mary, Queen of Love
      Who never questioned why —

D etours may obstruct the way —
      let's face truth and never hide
      By honesty she lived her days —
      Let Chrissy be our guide.

Do not cry for too long for she loves to hear us laugh —
I promised her I'd tell you all of this on her behalf.

                    Love, Kathie

Bored?

B etter to learn how to knit and sew
O r a hobby like crosswords – to take where you go
R eading and writing and drawing are fun
E ven puzzles and games are for most everyone
D on't depend on technology is what this is about

(You can still use a candle when the power is out!)

Maturity

M aking the most of your
A ssets and attributes
T houghtfully and tenaciously
U nselfishly utilizing
R ealistic rules with
I nspiration and intelligence
T urning – in time to be
Y our best self.

Secrets

There's a forest in my heart
Where I sometimes go to find me
On a carpet of pine needles
I am softened as I run.
And the chattering of tree dwellers
So cheerfully surrounds me
And contentment and my spirit join as one.

There's a lake behind my eyes
I can go to when I close them
To refresh within her waters
And to rest upon her shore.
I can bask in meditation
While the sun melts down behind her
With today dissolving into evermore.

There's a mountain in my memory
I envision when I need to
Feel the strength of something bigger
Next to ordinary me.
If it doesn't serve the purpose
Overshadowing anxiety –
I simply then depict it near the sea.

There's a child in my person
Always eager to delight me
Joyful in anticipation
That I might come in and play.
Still alive with lilting Laughter
Filled with fantasy and frolic

And I pray that she will never go away. – 1989

Respect

R – Remember – we are

E – Equals!

S – Standing together as

P – Partners

E – Each one

C – Contributing 100%

T – Together.

Wisdom

W orking towards
I nner peace and
S elf
D efinition, while
O vercoming
M adness!

July 2005

What Is...

Looking for the goodness
Overlooking much
Validating qualities
Emphasizing touch

Love, Mom

Wordsense

C – Caring
O – Overlooking
M – Mentoring
P – Pardoning
A – Assisting
S – Soothing
S – Securing
I – Influencing
O – Ongoing
N – Necessary!

R – Reasoning and
E – Expecting that by
S – Sympathizing, you're
C – Convincing someone to change –
U – Using up your own resources on an
E – Endless voyage.

One is born of angst –
Feverish from the start.
The other blossoms freely –
As love does – from the heart.

Depression

D istance
E volves,
P aralyzing
R elationships,
E motional
S uffering
S tagnates, in
I ntensely
O verwhelming
N egativity.

Enabler

E – Enough is enough of
N – Not speaking my mind!
A – Always trying to
B – Believe that I'm just being kind!
L – Love should empower us, not be an
E – Excuse for escaping
R – Reality by power misuse!!

Resolution

There's a great big something missing
Like a deep dark empty hole
Emotions pulled out by the roots
Way down in my soul.

I cannot make sense of conditions
Wasted tears and years asking why
I keep launching kites, just not to look down
Tripping over myself as I try.

I am guilty of screwing up plenty
While doing my dance 'round the pit
Don't know if I'll ever be rescued
Should I topple and fall into it.

It's a race to make up for my losses
Biting off much more than I chew
Even when life's at its fullest –
Underneath lies that emptiness too.

So I'll dance with a feverish spirit
Pray intensely whenever I'm still
Fearlessly love and do good
And vow that forever I will.

11–12–05

Advice

Keep your nose in the flowers
Keep your toes in the grass
Drink the pleasures of the seasons
Taste the days before they pass!

Fix your eyes above the treetops
Feel your face upon the breeze
Bathe in raindrops and in sunbeams
Matters most – that which will please!

Saturate your ears with music
Press a song close to your lips
Teach your fingers tender touching
Dance before the movement slips!

Such a Precious Moment Life Is
Catch a ride upon its wing
Bear the turbulence of time –
With the Honey comes the Sting!!

Advice (2005)

A ll living creatures are due your respect
D o unto others as you would expect
V alue the universe – especially the earth
I mprove where you are – to determine your worth
C onsciously act – and mind what you say
E very night bow your head to Our Father and pray.

July 2005

Children Play

Children play – It is their nature
Morning, afternoon and night.
Sometimes stop to make a picture
It's their world – and all is right!

Children let their spirits shine!
We have long forgotten how
Everything to them is fine
Celebrating in the now.

Children are in sync with angels –
They sing and dance and flap their wings!
Elicit smiles and winks from strangers
Touched by the grace a child brings

Children look for our approval –
Busy lives stand in the way
Obstacles for our removal!
Love insurance day by day,

Children playing are the teachers!
Making angels in the snow
"A child shall lead them," quote the preachers
We are learning – as they grow!!

When children play – we are their servants
Take the time to smile and wink!
Participate by our observance –
To Heaven they remain our link!!

03–19–09

Kathie's Commencement Poem – May 1999 (Whew!)

How did I do it – you all want to know
Well I had LOTS OF HELP on the way
Like from Paul who was there to support me
By pitching in at home every day.

He does dishes you know and the laundry
He vacuums and makes the cars run
In spite of the work-load he carries
He ALWAYS makes time for some fun.

Like movies and dinner and dancing
He knows how to help me unwind
And all that he ever had asked in return...
Is EVERY SUNDAY – HIS PASTA ON TIME!!

I had lots of help too from some others
Like Tara and Dorothy and Eileen
Who helped me research – and took me to church
And typed and re-typed while I screamed!

To the Capos who kept sending food
And to Jean who made sure I got out-some
To the friends who's calls I sometimes didn't return
Thanks for 'hangin in' when my friendship seemed
doubt-some

To Tammy who got me through Science
And Catherine who got me through 'Stats'
To Kathy, Chris and Tara – who kept me out walkin'
To keep me from growin' too fat(s)!

To my family and friends who stood by me
While I moaned and complained – even cried
It's important you're all here together
So you don't think I simply just lied.

With the cap and the gown as my proof
And the ink on my degree hardly dry
I don't know what I'll have to complain about now
Still – I'll give it the 'old college try'!!

FOR PAULIE AND MARCI AND MARC AND LUKE
YOU'RE THE REASON I HAD TO SUCCEED
FOR I WANTED TO SHOW YOU WHAT
PERSISTENCE CAN DO
NOT BY TELLING YOU – BUT BY SHOWING YOU
IN DEED

THANK YOU ALL! THANK YOU EVER SO MUCH!!
I don't know where I'm goin' from here
–But if anyone knows of a PUBLIC SCHOOL JOB –
Say the word – and I'll buy you a beer!!!

With Love,
Kathleen M. Rizzo B.A. Elem Ed. B.S. Soc. Ass. Ear.
Chld.
(…and I can belly dance!)

Riverdance – 2006

As a Pisces I've always acknowledged
That water is steadfast the theme
Rivers and Oceans and Lakes
Uplifting my life it would seem.

Thus the 'grande–finale' of Summer
Was kissed by the clouds and the sun
As gladly I welcomed the challenge
Of swimming the Hudson for fun.

I did it for M.S. last Summer
The current – a difficult test
Took 2:37 to make it across
I really gave it my best.

As a fool – I just love a good challenge
Leukemia – this year the cause
With last year's swim a success
I accepted with hardly a pause.

Recalling the day as it went
Allow me to say from the start
After viewing the waves from the bridge
Should have cancelled – if I had been smart!

This year the waters were swifter
The temperature also was colder
The waves were relentlessly fierce!
 And me – a whole 'nother year older!!

Adventurers – we in the river
Nature and Spirits as One
Counting the reasons to fail
We agreed that the total was – none!

Thus I broke into the waters
Back into the womb for rebirth
Pushing my way with intensity
To labor for all I am worth!

Intimacy with the Hudson
Leaves no time for cuddling up
Aggressive bed-fellow – the river
A battle for who stays on top!

I barely kept head above water
Felt much like an overturned sloop!
Repeatedly taking the punches
And frequently knocked for a loop!!

Determined and kicking with force
Exerting to find my next breath
Seemingly haphazard strokes
Rhythmless – dancing with death!

"Heaven help me!" – I cried in my head!
But the river kept slapping my face!
"Whatever could I have been thinking? –
To make me enter this race?!!"

I hardly look much like a mermaid –
More like 'The Old Man and the Sea'
Who is that Granny out there on the river?
Just brazen and pitiful me!!

Breathing became an ordeal
As the whitecaps I swallowed up whole
Gasping in water – not air
Ingesting with little control.

"What the hell am I drinking?!" I panicked
P.C.B.'s cannot be a good thing!!
I might wake up Mutant tomorrow
With a fin! Or a bill! Or a wing!!

As my life passed before me I reckoned
In the future it just might behoove
Thinking twice before swimming the Hudson
Reconsidering what I must prove!

For I ain't getting any too younger
As you know that I'm sure no 'Spring Chicken'
My head is in need of examining
Volunteering to take such a lickin'!!!

I finished in 2:12 this time
With the undertow making me bonkers!!
Swept me right past my destination –
And carried me nearly to Yonkers!!!

I had to depend on the kindness
And skills of a man in a kayak
Who bid me hang on as he struggled
In order to safely return back!

With my arms all Vaselined up
Holding on to the boat was a battle!
I held on for dear life to my hero
While he struck at the waves with each paddle!!

The powerful river defied us
I even slipped off once or twice
It was awesome to me – his persistence
And that a stranger could be so nice.

Brought me safely back where I belonged
Determined he was to deliver
He told me his name was Mike –
My St. Michael Archangel of the River!!

So alas I am here to retell it
Mike's rowing ensured my arrival!
Last year I felt much like "Rocky"
This year it was more like "Survival!!"

Thanks to all those who supported
My efforts with a check or a prayer
www.lls.org/wchswin
Will recreate it as if you were there!

When viewing the photos of swimmers
You'll see me there looking real cute!
With my pink bathing cap and broad hips –
In the black skirted granny-type suit!!!

Enjoy!! Thanks again!! Love, thekath

7. FRIENDS

Prayer For Jean – Love, Kathie

Jean, my very dearest friend,
Has a problem with one end –
While out one night to celebrate –
Must be something that she ate!
And now she pays the awful price –
And for sure it isn't very nice!
How did that dirty damn bacterier –
Get inside so very near to her!

She's been through so much wear and tear –
So it really doesn't seem quite fair!
Please let the doctors find the source –
To kill the bug that is the cause!

So Jean can get back in the swing –
And back to doing everything!
She needs to work and play and dance!
Go out with friends in her sparkly pants!!

She can't be laid up 'under the weather' –
Oh please God help to make her better!
She's mine and everybody's friend!
Please calm her intestines so they can mend!

Please make her well – we really need her!
She's always been our fearless leader!!
Our social director – our dancing queen! –
Our party planner – our dear friend Jean!!

Please make her well and keep her happy –
Thy will be done – but please make it snappy!
Amen.   07–26–21

Roses and Lilacs

My friend Jean who lives next door –
Is such an inspiration!
She demonstrates that life is for –
A daily celebration!!

She's always up to something –
She's as busy as a bee!
In the yard a-puttering –
Or on a shopping spree!!

Cooking up a storm –
After cleaning out the cellar
In her kitchen nice and warm –
With John who is her fella!!

On a Sunday after church –
It's a regular routine
Show a man his worth –
With home cooking served by Jean!

Actively she comes and goes –
In daytime and at night
Upkeeps her pace and rarely slows –
Weekdays, weekends, despite!

She loves her time with baby –
Her newest little grandson!
She's right, I don't mean maybe –
Little Salvatore is handsome!!

She rises up to meet them –
Whenever family calls
At her table she will greet them –
With a platter of meatballs!!

She has had a lot of birthdays –
But she doesn't show her age
Face and figure still worth-praise –
In her 60's I would wage.

(But that's not why I'm writing –
I digress – so let's go on
It's to friendship I'm reciting –
or a blessing like a mom!)

On the coldest morning –
Still goes out to shovel snow!
And when the days are warming –
She makes the flowers grow!!

Over the fence or over tea –
To visit is a pleasure!
Sharing stories, she and me –
Our friendship is a treasure!!

Though on the road of life –
She has had her ups and downs
Overcoming every strife –
Her spirit still abounds!

Such a lovely person –
Whose experience of dread
Could have left her cursing –
Chose the opposite instead.

Her disposition never shows –
She carries many crosses
In her heart a garden grows –
Covering up her losses.

Raking in the Autumn –
Out shoveling in the cold
Recovering when she's fallen –
No such thing as growing old!!

In the sun where I am lazing –
I look up from my book
The woman is amazing –
Up to elbows in yard-work!!

She runs circles around most –
In all kinds of weather!
And she's still 'feeling her oats' –
Not getting older, but just better!!

She's broken bones and twisted ankles! –
But she's never given up!!
Just went home and took two Advils –
When run over by a truck!!!

She's a beacon of endurance –
Just like Lady Liberty!
Ever steady through the currents –
With strength and sensitivity.

Her stamina inspires me –
The 'Ever Ready Bunny'!
Keeps on giving tirelessly –
And warm as tea with honey!!

Gives me Roses in the Summertime –
And Lilacs in the Spring
Appreciates my every rhyme!
And shares her everything.

A neighbor to rely on –
A friend for every season
A shoulder I can cry on –
Or have tea with when it's freezin'!!

The ins and outs of many years –
Has let our friendship grow
Roses, Lilacs, laughter, tears –
Are lessons we both know.

This woman is a blessing –
And she probably doesn't know it
And so I am addressing her –
This time as a poet!

She is a friend indeed –
For she always takes the time
To listen to me read –
So I dedicate this rhyme

Through life and love she labors –
To her garden she attends
God has made us neighbors –
And love has made us friends.

Ladies of Liberty

Women in White
Comrades in the night
Weathering the storm
Pieta – in uniform

Symbol of all good
Purity of Motherhood
Lilies in the rain
Kindlers of the flame

Seekers in the dark
Sheltering the spark
Loyal to the past
Make the future last!

1991

Dear Mayor and Mrs. Presto

Here's to the Gentleman Mayor
And here's to his Great Lady Kaye!
To the Host and the Hostess of Carlstadt
There are things we've long wanted to say.

Your stature and presence among us
We've taken for granted too long.
It's time that we honor your greatness
With a verse or appropriate song.

There's a special dimension you've added
To the title of Mayor and Wife
An example of community kinship
You've inspired to all... by your life.

With your generous hearts and strong spirits
What a lasting impression you've made.
Be assured you have touched many lives
Through the courage you both have displayed.

The light from the love in your family
Can illuminate all of this town!
Sincerity shines in your smiles
Not a trace of your hardship is found.

Hats off from your good-hearted people!
For whom you have always been there.
Instead of a poem or a ballad –
We'll honor you both with a prayer.

Our Father Who art truly in Heaven
We in Carlstadt have something to say.
Please watch over our Great Mayor Presto
And continue to bless Lady Kaye.

Amen.

07-10-90

Carry on Mayor!

To the Distinguished Mayor Presto
"The Silver Fox," named Dominick –
What kind of man is this mayor?
What kind of stuff makes him tick?

Twenty years he has held the position
A sign from the people he serves.
Tonight let us stand in ovation –
For the love and acclaim he deserves.

His people are precious to him
That's why he shows up everywhere.
For weddings and funerals and Girl Scouts,
Dependable Dom will be there.

At awards and parades and at dinners
Football games and Senior events,
Devoted and steadfast you'll find him
Our Mayor – Our Friend – no pretense.

"The man with nine lives" – some have called him.
God has blessed him again and again.
With the love and support of his family and
The esteem of both women and men.

Heart and soul he's devoted to Carlstadt,
Side by side with the strength of his wife.
Twenty years of hard work and long hours –
What a mark he has made with his life!

His has not been a carefree existence.
We all share in our hearts his endurance.
We are certain God's Graces are with him,
Along with our prayers – for insurance.

In '72 – '92 – or 2000!
He's the man that the people will choose.
So – Carry on Mayor Dominick Presto –
For there's no one to fit in your shoes!!

02-20-92

Welcome Home Mr. Capo!

What a wonderful man, Mr. Capo!
Dear Brother – and Father – and Friend
Life-mate Husband to Dolly
Devoted to her to the end.

Lived his life to the fullest!
What an example to us
Worked long and hard for his family
With never a regret or a fuss.

Always took time out for fun!
Whether bowling or down at the track
Took pride in his sparkling pool
And his bountiful garden out back.

He shared – and he shared – and he shared!
His pool and his vegetables too
Made the Greatest Pasta Fazool
Even better than Emeril could do.

And when the music was playing!
Who can forget – oh-by-golly
Those two gliding around just like pros
On the dance floor with Angelo and Dolly!!

Recalling this Wonderful Man!
Gratefulness enters my mind
In addition to qualities mentioned –
Like Generosity and just being Kind –

He's one of the last of Our Heroes!
Who served Bravely in World War II
Awarded the Purple Heart
His Courage was Tried and True!!

– And, He took on the Rizzos as Family!
And treated them just as his own
God Welcome Our Dear Mr. Capo!!
Returned to his Heavenly Home.

Heaven Sent!

Such a precious miracle –
this special little boy!
Baby Rafaelle –
you have filled our hearts with JOY!!

Irresistible – those cheeks!
For kissing and caressing!
Heaven sent you from above –
bestowed on us this blessing!!

The love you brought into our lives –
I cannot even measure!
I smile just to think of you! –
My Grandson, you're a Treasure!!

When I see your little face –
There's so much I am wishing –
Can't wait 'til you're a Yankee fan –
Can't wait to take you fishing!!

You fill our lives with so much love –
each time we see you smile –
We hope you don't grow up too fast –
Stay little for a while!

Your presence in our family –
has inspired all our roles –
As Parents and Grandparents –
You have touched our hearts and souls!

Your Mom will teach you wrong from right –
and how to be a gent –
Your dad will teach you music –
show you every instrument!

The extra love and lessons –
We are here to hereby grant –
From your Grandma and your Grandpa –
and your favorite Uncle and Aunt!

And with two sets of grandparents –
you're a lucky little lad! –
To be twice as blessed with love –
by your Nan and your Grandad!!

Our hearts are filled with Gratitude –
that Heaven sent you here –
That we have been entrusted
with a little man so dear!

We wish you Health and Happiness –
may Love surround you always –
May His Holy Spirit guide you –
and follow – all your days!

With Lots of Love,
Grandma and Grandpa

Man's Best Friend

Who asks for so little –
And gives so much more
Daily welcomes you home –
When you walk through the door
Is always forgiving –
When you're moody or cross
Will drop what he's doing –
for a quick game of toss
Who worships you just –
for a romp in the park
Is content just to lay –
by your feet in the dark
Respects your opinion –
when you're wrong or you're right
And alerts you to things
that go Bump in the night!
Who's loving – and faithful –
When you're up or you're down
Even longs to be near –
in spite of your frown!
When the world seems against you –
And you've nothing to spend
Who'll still Love and Adore you?
Only Man man's Best Friend –
(oh... and your wife !!)

How Lovely!!!

What a lovely gesture!
What a lovely gift!
Once again you've managed –
to give my heart a lift!!

I love the lovely statue –
of the lovely poet!
You make me feel so special –
with thoughtful ways to show it!!

(And thank you for your 'thank you'!
I loved the choreography!!
You really are creative! –
I'm glad you think so much of me!!)

I plan to make a special place –
to write when I retire –
And there upon a proper shelf –
the statue will inspire!!

So someday when I'm famous –
and my writing is well known –
I'll display my lovely statue –
in a museum to be shown!!!

'Til then it's in its place to –
make me smile and give me pleasure –
Another lovely symbol of your friendship –
which I treasure!!!

With lots of love dear friend

A Birthday Chorus for Dear Dolores!

It's time to raise our glasses for a lady –
A woman who is always 'on the go!'
We can't believe that she is turning 80! –
On her, the number really doesn't show!!

She's everybody's friend – Dolores McGuire! –
Serves in many clubs all over town
A busy gal, who never seems to tire –
Even knee replacement doesn't keep her down!!

She eagerly takes on most any job –
In Women's Club or Rosary Society Leader
As President of the Seniors Friendship Club –
She gives her time to anyone who needs her!

With all the talents that she can perform –
Like cooking for a crowd or baking cakes
She really is a cut above the norm! –
Puts lots of love in everything she makes!!

The culinary list goes on and on –
Her Carrot cake and Scones – the Best we know!
Especially her Eggplant Parmesan! –
Why she should probably have a cooking show!!

And never has there been a better neighbor! –
Generosity is just her style!!
You can always count on her to do a favor –
'At your service' and always with a smile!

Forever willing and never out of reach –
To lend a hand or just to have some fun!
(Some say that she likes "Sex on the Beach" –
A party girl when all is said and done!!)

Oh and by the way we've heard the dirt –
From some little town way down in Mexico
With a certain Native waiter she did flirt! –
Well there's a side of her we did not know!!

She's Bold! With Versatility!! –
Isn't gonna let life pass HER by!!
Doesn't waste an opportunity –
To play up to a handsome guy!!

You go girl!! – You are a true Red Hatter!! –
"Love 'em and leave 'em" down in Mexico!
Let them talk! – It really doesn't matter! –
Handsome waiters will come and go!!

Your reputation's safe back here in town –
(Everyone deserves a little 'fling!')
If in Mexico you clowned around –
Here in Carlstadt your praises we still sing!

–And why? Because you are our Special Friend –
You can't help it if you've got good looks!
Besides, no one else could ever take your place –
A gal who volunteers and bakes and cooks!!

Uh-oh – This was meant to be a toast! –
We wanted to salute you as our Friend!
Instead, it's turned into a roast! –
But we know our sense of humor you'll defend!

For what we most admire in your behalf –
Of all the qualities that you display
We love your smile and we love your laugh! –
The genuine love that you always convey!!

So Happy 80th Birthday dear Dolores! –
You've got a lot of livin' yet to do!
Now it's time to all join in the chorus! –
And sing the Happy Birthday song to you!!

My Dear Friend Pat

My dear friend Pat raised three fine men –
The treasures of her Life!
Present in the good times, then
Through obstacles and strife.

She labored so intensely –
And daily towed the line
She loved her sons Immensely!
And that Love will Always Shine!!

With Fortitude in Faith and Love
She bravely stayed the course
And held her ground from 'push to shove'
With Grace her only Force.

For those three sons she kept on track
And to her Faith held tight!
Not falling off while looking back
Remaining in their sight.

The anguish she has suffered through
A Sacrament estranged
The trials and guilt they never knew
She wished things could have changed.

Her family's what it's all about
By Love for them she's driven
With heart and soul she reaches out
And asks to be forgiven.

The total picture clarified
In light of Holy Truth
From Honesty – she never shied
The price of Heavenly worth!

In the moments I spent with her
She spoke mostly of her Boys
This I promised to deliver –
YOU ARE HER ETERNAL JOYS!!

A Most Outstanding Teacher!
To St. Joseph's – gave her Best!
High Standards were her feature
With scores above the rest!!

At 3:00 – with school dismissed
Available for sharing
A Confidant and Therapist
Her eyes True-Blue with caring.

Her Friendship is Indelible
As lasting as the sun
Her appetite Incredible
For Laughter and for Fun!!

Just an ordinary woman
Yet a Loving Inspiration!
By example she has proven
Heaven is our destination!

In turbulence it's hard to see –
But when the storm has calmed
On sunny days for you and me
Fond Memories are warmed.

I look to sunny days ahead –
For Pat and for us all
By her Love-light we will be led
And in our faith stand Tall!!

With Unending Love and Friendship,
Kathie Rizzo 03–11–10

To Patricia

Good Friends
Compliment each other
In the sun
One a shade of red
The other brown.
Good Friends
Play beneath the sun
And laugh
And shout!
Their voices echo one.
But two distinct and natural smiles
Glow
The gift of Friendship is
Renewed
With each new sun.
The smile –
The guarantee that
Marks Good Friends.

Good Friends
Huddle close in times of storm
Secure themselves
With coffee and a glance.
When thunder breaks
Good Friends – wait
And watch
And wonder
Why and when
Together.
Then sit in silence still
And sigh

And see
The earth and one another's hearts.

Good Friends
Sing beneath the night
And know each other's songs
Both sad – and gay
And harmonize
And laugh between.
And time cannot touch Good Friends.
There is no fatality
The world can inflict
For each Friend is a healer
Of the other.
And all the earth in splendor
And all the glorious skies
All rest in calm tranquility
And nod in envy when they see –
Good Friends.

Kathie Pell 1967

Read to Me

Come
And take a place beside me
While the earth still emanates
The last warm breath of summer.
Here
On the ebb of changing seasons
While the concert of the earth subsides
Take virtuoso now – my friend
And read to me.

Now
While the earth is standing still
And fading
In its final muted green –
Losing contrast with the sky
Before it's rusty and defeated
'Neath the greedy bleaching sun.
Come – my friend
And read to me.

My words lay lifeless in obscurity
On their paper shroud
Unsung
They are the requiem of my soul.
Revive them now I pray you
Breathe my words
In wedding with your voice.
Come
Messiah of my mind
And bathe the oozing self within me
With your soothing serenade.

Preserve the sweetness of sincerity
With the seasoning of your ways.
Share in the feast
Which my heart has prepared.
You are the connoisseur of my words
So come my friend
And read to me.

Kathie Pell 1968

Triplet Timeline

Back in October of '99 –
the Triplets made their debut!
Tara and Chris came through it just fine –
two Sons and one Daughter, brand new!!

Then came the diapers and feedings and baths –
Family and friends were so good!
24/7 of crying and laughs –
and grabbing some sleep when they could!!

The very First Birthday came up mighty fast –
A big celebration they had!
Three Healthy Triplets – through Babyhood passed –
and everyone just felt so glad!!

Next they were Toddlers – then 'Terrible Twos' –
The Triplets grew smarter and cuter!
Daily they practiced the "Don't"s and the "Do"s –
With Tara and Mother and Tutor!!

As they got older, they traveled real well –
so off to the seashore they went!
Aunts, Uncles and Cousins and all of the Grells –
Family vacations well spent!!

Thriving and Happy and Healthy and Strong –
Look at the Three of Them now!
Loving and Loveable for all the days long –
Tara and Chris – take a bow!!!

Grandmas and Grandpas both here and in Heaven –
are as Pleased and as Proud as can be!
Blessed with the Families that they have been given –
sprouting New – From the Old Family Tree!!

It's thanks to their Steadfast Example –
of Faithfulness right to the end!
Celebrations like this are a sample –
To Spiritual Growth we must tend!!

See how Their Goodness remained! –
The tradition of Faith carries on!
By habits and rituals maintained –
Long after Elders are gone!!

Ask Tara and Chris how they get through each day –
and they'll tell you face to face –
They always take the time out to Pray –
acknowledging His Holy Grace!!

The Sacraments still remain Sacred –
just as a Family's Love –
A retreat from all sin and hatred –
Instituted by Heaven Above!!

So 'Come Lord Jesus' – Come today! –
To Michael and James and Erin!
Your Holy Presence again will convey –
The Gift of Faith that they share–in!!

God Bless Michael, James and Erin on your First
Communion Day and Always!

Happy 50th Anniversary Eddie and Ena!!!

'Twas 50 short years ago
A couple that you and I know
Fell madly and gladly in love
And were blessed by the heavens above!

In the Land of the Wee Leprechaun
They became Mr. and Mrs. Moran
Then off to the grand U.S.A.
And still happily married today!

Their lives have been hectic and busy
With schedules that make most folks dizzy
Yet, if you happen to drop in to see –
They'll make you a nice pot of tea!

With so many kids and grandkids
You'd think they'd be out of their wits
But life is well balanced instead
With enough love from Ena and Ed!

That Eddie's a talented feller
Taxidermist and great storyteller
He thrives on his family and pets
The more work – the younger he gets!

He's still such a good looking stallion
That he's often mistook for Italian
With that thick hair so wavy and dark
On Ena's heart he left his mark!

After 9 kids – what's the chance
For Ena to paint and to dance
Even took up college classes
And with flying colors – she passes!

Still the prettiest woman I've ever seen
Once Ireland's own beauty queen
She greets everyone with a smile
Always eager to chat for a while!

With such lovely skin and great hair
You'd think that she hadn't a care
Effervescent those sparkling blue eyes
No wonder she became Eddie's prize!

In marriage there's laughter and tears
But they weathered the storms through the years
By their faith they respond to the call
They're an inspiration to us all!

To the couple that never looks tired
By your family and friends you're admired
For Eddie and Ena so dear
We raise up our glasses to cheer!

May your turmoil and troubles be few
May your hand-holding love remain new
So the Moran family name never ends
And for 50 more years we stay friends!!

HAPPY GOLDEN ANNIVERSARY
TO A GOLDEN COUPLE!!!!!!!!!!!!!!!

Helene is 60!!!

Our dear Helene is 60!
Let's have a glass of wine!
It seems like only yesterday
That she was 59!!

Our friend Helene is 60!
Let's pour another glass!
How does she stay so young?
Her face – her waist – her a-ttitude!!

It must be from her love-life
Or her travels all about
Or is her beauty secret
Simply that she's still a scout!!

Hooray! Helene is 60!
Let's have another round!
If growing old's a problem
The solution we have found!

Let's vow to stay together
And merrily drink and eat!
And celebrate these birthdays
With our tired dancing feet!!

Yes – Helene is 60!
And tonight she's having fun!!
It's a pity she might not remember
Tomorrow when the partying's done!!

Helene's lucky to be 60!
No more flashes – no more sweats!
With a bottle of red and white and us
This is probably as good as it gets!!

These birthdays just keep coming!
My how the time does fly!!
There's just one way to welcome them
So raise your glasses high!!!

HAPPY BIRTHDAY DEAR HELENE!
And many-many more!
And now we want a piece of cake
Cuz that's what friends are for!!!!!

To the Golden Girls!

We are the Golden Girls –
We're Sixty and Seventy and Sassy!
We've practiced at life for so long that,
We're Charming and Clever and Classy!!

Experience has been a good teacher,
So we're Wise and we're Tough and we're Strong!
We've all been around a few blocks –
Mostly in New Jersey – where we belong.

On the bumpy old highway of life,
We've handled the potholes just fine.
There's nothing we can't overcome –
With a song and a laugh and some wine!

The first of our credits goes like this –
Raised some kids, and have friends that adore us!
Loved and served both our family and friends,
And cherished the ones gone before us.

We are blessed by our Great dispositions!
Our ability to Laugh and to Love!!
We're commissioned to instigate Joy –
By that Big Laughmaker Above!!!

We are the Golden Girls!
For our hearts are made truly of Gold!!
And we can drink and dance better than
twenty-year-olds –
So don't think for a minute we're Old!!!!!!!!!!!!!!!!!!!!!!!

2003

260

Audrey's Smile

St. Mary's High School – Sophomore year
I was the new kid in school.
In Geometry class I sat in the rear –
(Math made me feel like a fool!)

It was way back in 1963
I just moved into town
I didn't know them – and they didn't know me –
So I mostly just looked down.

Ten minutes into Geometry –
I ventured to look around
The teacher – a threatening figure he!
And no one was making a sound.

How will I ever get through this class?!
I felt like my nerves were on trial!!
I don't think I'll be able to pass!
– Just then she gave me her smile.

She whispered to me, "Oh good grief!" –
This Geometry stuff is unreal!!"
I agreed and thought – what a relief!
Someone who feels like I feel!!!

"Hi – I'm Audrey – And you must be Kathie"
She smiled and said, "glad to know you!"
The first friendly person I'd seen!
It's hard to make friends when you're so new.

It's uncomfortable on the first day
– But with Audrey that wasn't the case –
With her friendly and outgoing way –
And that Beautiful Smile on her face!

Sitting through class was a chore!
But Audrey made being there – Fun!!
We didn't know what was in store –
Lifelong friendship when it was done.

Together we got through the class –
A wonderful friendship occurred –
She DID – but I DIDN'T pass!
And she comforted me when she heard.

All I recall from Geometry –
Is that a circle never ends –
Much like the circle of life –
And the love of our family and friends.

After High School we went separate ways –
Then met up again some years after
Life is hard – but my friend Audrey says –
Still ready with smiles and with laughter.

When I was the new kid in town
She was the First Friend I made!
With marriages and children now grown –
For 46 years Friends we've stayed!!

What a Blessing to have such a friend!
Who suffered – and yet all the while –
Inspired us right 'til the end!
By keeping her faith – and her smile.

Her journey on earth now has ended
(We are only here for a while)
I am grateful for the day she befriended –
– And I'll never forget Audrey's smile.

06–10–09

Dear Friend Geri – Love Kathie

I am so sorry for your pain –
I hope you'll soon be yourself again!
I wish I could help the way you've helped me –
On my rosary I pray that you'll be pain-free!
Growing older, these things come and go –
And you're such a fighter we already know!
You are loved by so many who support you right now
– with meds and therapy
And good doctors' 'know-how'!
For all you have done and for all that you do –
I'm just one of your friends who are grateful for you!!
Let's all join in spirit and love and in prayer –
And picture you, dear friend, poolside in your chair!
Just take some deep breaths and close your eyes –
Can you taste the wine – can you visualize?
Can you hear the laughs – can you feel the freeze? –
Can I give you a refill? – pass the chips and dip please!
Sending positive thoughts that can turn into real! –
Happy memories – coupled with faith that can heal!!
Faith is more than a mental doodle! –
It will keep you a-float like a Styrofoam 'noodle'!
Hold on tight and keep right on kickin'! –
You've taken a lickin' but you'll keep right on tickin'!!
For along with the doctors and therapies –
Faith and laughter - still the best cure under the trees!
So I'm printing some really good laughs from the 'net'
And saving to share them for the best summer yet!
Better days lie ahead I am already smiling –
With Josh – Chardonnay – and Pinot's stockpiling!
I'm sending you this 'poem' to show how much I care!
I'm feeling well enough to come –
Just call and I'll be there!!

Dear Lynne

What on earth did you do to your wrist?
While dancing around your pool!
We are much too old to be doing the twist –
In an effort to prove we're still cool!

You really have done it this time!
Thank God 'twas your left that got broke –
We all think we are still in our prime –
But a trip by the pool is no joke!!

Next don't you be thinkin' 'bout cartwheels!
Or you'll really be pushing your 'luck'
Imagine how a second fall feels –
How both right and left wrist-less would suck!!

Use this time wisely and rest now!
Let others step up to the plate –
Do whatever one arm will allow –
The TV remote's a good mate!!!

It's ok to sip tea on your couch –
In the morning watching 'Drew' and 'The View' –
Self-healing doesn't make you a 'slouch!'
You know first you must take care of you!!

We have all now arrived at the crossroads –
A time to refresh and restore!
So far we have balanced the boatloads –
And are willing to do even more!!

But please let us pause and take heed!
Remember what we learned as a scout –
'Be prepared!' – keep your phone where you need!
Especially when you have to step out!

I do hope your wounds now are mending –
So as friends we can gather real soon!
That your story will have a happy ending –
Way before the ending of June!!

Love & prayers and lol's – thekath
XOXOXOXOXOXOXXO
PS...Written on my couch w/TV on mute! :)

Sister Shirley's Golden Jubilee – 2006!!

Come one and come all!
Come late or come early!
Come help us to celebrate
Our dear Sister Shirley!!

Come dance and come sing!
Come cry happy tears!
She's been serving The Lord
For Fifty Good Years!!

Through some ups and some downs
(And sometimes upside down!)
She's lived up to the Gospel
In many a town.

For gladly she traveled
Where The Spirit would take her
Even served the good folks
Way down in Jamaica!!

From New York to New Jersey
To Florida and Mass.
You just never know in –
Which direction she'll pass!

Where can she be now?
Many times we're not sure –
Then 'knock-knock' – SURPRISE!
There she is at the door!!

Suitcase in hand –
And that Big Shirley Grin!
After such a long time!!
Sometimes Years it has been!!!

For she'll drive a long distance
No matter how far –
Just to visit with friends
With the lend of a car!!

Happy Golden Jubilee!
To a Real Golden-Girl!!
May God Always Bless You –
Our Dear Sister Shirl!!!

Hail Mary for Audrey

Hail Mary full of grace
Comfort Audrey in your embrace
The Lord is with Thee
And Blessed art Thou
Rain down Your blessings
To heal Audrey now.

Among all women
God chose You above others
As a Beacon of Guidance
Especially to mothers.
Blessed is Jesus, The Fruit of Your Womb
With Your intercession
Audrey's health can re-bloom!

Dear Holy Mary
Mother of God
Smile down on Audrey
To our request – Give a nod.
Pray for us sinners
Now and at the hour
Of our death – but for now
Hear all of the power –
Of Love from our prayers
As we beseech you this night
To heal Audrey's cancer
By the faith we hold tight! Amen.

Roasting The Rev!

Some say "the Donald"
Some say "the Rev."
Some may call him "the Pastor"
He is seen all around – walking all over town
(But I think that he used to walk faster!)

Maybe the dog's getting younger!
Or maybe his shoes are too tight!
Whatever the reason – in any season –
He's out walking both day and night.

You'll know him when you see him
By a colorful hat or tie
And an outstanding shirt – or a Plaid Pleated Skirt!!
With his knee-socks pulled way up high!

And when he's not out walking
He also likes to ride
In limos and on motorcycles
Or hanging on a fire truck's side!

At a party or celebration
Or sorting event or rally
He's right in the crowd – often singing out loud!
Right next to the ear of his Sally!!

He loves to say grace at a function
He's even been known to sing it!!
Even in a pinch – telling jokes is a cinch!
He'll just get right up there and wing it!!

Even when he's at a funeral
He manages to make people smile
He is there to remind us – to put sorrow behind us
Uplighting our spirits – in style!!

At St. Joe's they welcome him in
Even stands with the Priest at the pulpit
Always passes on the Bread – Takes the Wine cup
instead
But it's Holy – so why does he GULP it??!!!

And who knew that ministers dance??!!
Why he hardly can stay in his seat!!
When the Rev starts be-bopping – There's really no
stopping
His Wild Presbyterian feet!!!!

Such a fun-lovin' son-of-a-gun!!
I can say just one thing – that at least
He's a helluva guy – and he's not even high!
But it's a good thing that he's not a Priest!!!

Yes – everyone loves Revered Pitches
It's about time they gave you a Roast!
It was all just for fun – but you may want to run –
For when you get home – you are TOAST!!!!!

2004

Baby Jake's Christening Day – May 25, 2008

On this special day – we give thanks to God!
For big Sam's little brother – two peas in a pod!!

Jake is such a blessing! – Sam is such a joy!
Everybody welcomes – another Kimak boy!!

Congratulations Peter – and his lovely wife Michele!
For following the recipe – that you do so well!!

Children are a miracle – that only "he" can make!
Little Sam is wonderful! – and God bless little Jake!!

With lots of love,
The Rizzos

First Communion Day – May 3, 2008
From Michael, Erin and James

As a first communion keepsake
To slip in your favorite book
A marker we want you to take
To help find your page when you look!

This first communion day
Is also a 'marker' of sorts
A 'passage of rites' you could say
The essence of faith it supports.

The church in her love and wisdom
Chose Mary's month as the season
The children learned catechism
While approaching the age of reason.

Seeing this, think of their names
On their holiest day – you were there
For Michael and Erin and James –
We hope that you'll lift up a prayer.

Catching Up on Valor

Congratulations Robert!
You made the front page news!!
As Citizen and Veteran –
you've more than paid your dues!
In Viet Nam you served us well –
with Valor, Brave and Strong!
Sadly your recognition
was made to wait so long.
The wounds – Your Badge of Honor –
have carried you thus far.
Now finally, the Purple Heart! –
and the merited Bronze Star!!
You've carried on with Dignity –
Hard Working Family Man!
Strived to make an honest living
as a Good American!!
We salute you Mr. Milligan!
Your day at last has come!!
We're glad your name's not on That Wall –
still with us, not like some.
God Bless You for Your Service –
and for Your Sacrifice!
For these belated Medals –
You have More than paid The Price!!!

With Love and Gratitude,
The Rizzo Family

8. AUTUMN

Beginning Fall

Fat little robins – hopping on the lawn
Gathering instinctively – and soon they will be gone.

Crickets still in hiding – maintain a weary chant
While busy little squirrels – with acorns dig and plant.

Leaves in the treetops – green but not for long
Whisper weather changes – in an early Autumn song.

Each week a little cooler – than the week before
Temperatures revealing – what the season has in store.

09–30–10

Autumn in NY

Red, Orange, Gold and Brown, a bit of Green between

Trees in Autumn Glory – flaunting – begging to be seen!

A feast for free for us to see – with searching hungry eyes –

Consistent blessing on us all this Annual Surprise!

Inhaling October

Breathing in October air
On my usual night time walk –
Exhaling purges every care
Proceeding in the damp and dark.

Pumpkins on the porches grinning
Raked up leaf-piles by the curbs –
Desperate crickets' high notes crooning
In the silent night disturbs.

Unlikely still this Autumn evening
It's hardly Fall without a breeze –
Unloose the scarf I did not need bring
And deeply inhale as I please.

Just last month high in the trees
Fresh and green the canopy –
Now all papery the leaves
Crushed and crunching under me.

Pondering that Winter's near
It's Summer memories I treasure –
But Summer's gone and I'm still here
And every season has its pleasure

Conscious of my every breath
Taken in with gratitude –
Introspection to new depths
Refreshing change of attitude.

Inhale — exhale — let it go
Every step my thoughts renew –
Reconsidering what I know
Seasons change my point of view.

What will happen when I'm old
And no longer can walk outside?
Bundle me against the cold –
Open up the windows wide!

I will savor every season
Close my eyes and reminisce –
Of simple things in life most pleasing
A walk on Autumn nights like this.

10–26–08

Evening in Autumn

Serious winds are blowing
Giving Summer days the boot!
Acorns – Pumpkins – Chestnuts –
Enters Autumn – bearing fruit!

Colors twirling – colors dancing
Overhead and on the ground
Apples selling on the roadside –
By the bushel – or the pound.

Crickets – once in chorus
Now a solo serenade
Empty parks and beaches –
Where the Summer children played.

Past the rustling tree-tops
As they bid the last good-bye
A familiar farewell honking –
From the geese across the sky.

Evening time in Autumn
Smoking chimneys fill the air
Billowing thoughts of Summer –
When we did not have a care.

The Changing

Orange on the sidewalk
Golden on the ground
Brown and Crimson screaming –
With hardly any sound.

Swooshing winds deliver
Notices of Fall
Rusty notes – once Summergreen
Announcing Autumn's call.

Best to Savor Summer
And not give in to mourn
Welcome open-armed
The sibling season – as it's born.

October Eve

Crisp and cold the Autumn air
Slow the dying crickets' song
Hands in pockets – zippered jacket
Swift my sneakers move along.

Someone's fireplace is sending
Smokey messages that warn
Of impending weather changes
Frost on pumpkins in the morn'!

Once the treetops whispered soft
Raspy now – the drying leaves
Last week beheld the fading green
In realization my sad heart grieves.

But then the senses overtake
Inhaling deeply I embrace
Restorative – the Autumn air
Reminding me of Nature's Grace!

I never take for granted trees
Their influence my life defines
Trees and Sky – like character
True blue and evergreen as pines!

Autumn changes everything!
New season – new identity
Green releases red and gold
Tomorrows colorful and free!!

2007

Observing Autumn

A dash of Auburn/Orange –
A pinch of Crimson/Red
A sprinkling of Burgundy –
On the ground – a Golden spread!
Empty branches scratch the sky –
a stark reality –
A bold acceptance of the change –
stripped of Greenery.
The limbs outstretched and barren –
expose a squirrel's nest!
Below the trunk the raked leaves piled –
take up their Autumn rest.
Daring hawks extending wings
perform in fearless flight –
Bounce and frolic in the wind –
maneuvering with might!
The sky is mid-November Grey –
the chimney smoke adds to it –
The wind at night, a premonition –
that whispers 'Winter' through it.
Displays of vibrant mums and pumpkins
on the porch adorn –
While just across the highway
lay the leveled fields of corn.
Summer seems so far away –
a lovely memory –
I sense my own transition –
in the changing scenery.
And now I'm left to ponder –
empty trees, for months ahead –
Or – observe the earth's transitioning –
with wonderment instead! – 11-03-15

283

Awesome Autumn!

Piles and piles of leaves on the ground
Brown ones and orange and gold
Red and yellow still billowing down
Let loose by a wind-gust so bold.

Branches weave baskets against the sky
Void of a Summer once green
Beneath in a jacket and hood am I
Observing the Autmn scene.

Faintly the last of the crickets heard
Squirrels – busier than ever
High in the treetops the call of a bird
The chill in the air makes me shiver.

I scrunch up my shoulders, tuck in my chin
Brace for the change in the season
No turning back to the Summer that's been
Time to prepare for the freezing.

The birds and the crickets and the squirrels all know
They take the transition in stride
The trees remain standing long after the show
Of releasing their colors with pride.

Why do I fret about Winter?
The field-mouse just burrows and copes
All the while in the time I've spent here
Lofty evergreens guarding my hopes.

I notice them more with the leaves gone
Centurions silent and strong
Constant and steadfast and sure of the sun
I marvel as I walk along

Still the forest seems empty and bare
The treetops uncovered and raw
The luster is no longer there –
Yet – here I am standing in awe!

Hooked!

Hello – my name is Kathie
And I am addicted I fear
To an obsessive–compulsive behavior
That comes around just once a year.

I can't seem to stop myself
I'm totally out of control
Are there others who share my condition?
Has anyone taken a poll?

Maybe I'll start a support group
There must be "12 Steps" for our kind
I've decided to come out of the closet
To keep me from losing my mind!

When I see them I just can't resist
And I never can get quite enough
My family's caught on to my fetish
For in books they keep finding my "stuff!"

My husband finally frisked me
And found in my pockets and sleeves
The source of my Autumn Addiction –
An assortment of colorful leaves!

I set out for my exercise walks
But I can't keep my eyes off the ground
Soon my pockets and fists overflow
With the beautiful leaves that I found!

So much for aerobic attempts
My greedy eyes just look and look
Got to get those beauties home fast
And press 'em down quick in a book!

And the next day I'll do it again
And again and again 'til it rains
Is it possible my leaf-abuse habit
Can actually be frying my brains?!

Well – it only lasts for the season
When Wintertime comes I detox
By the Spring I am clean – but in Summer
On the beach I start picking up rocks!!

11–12–03

Driving Home

Circling hawk against the sky
Autumn patchwork mountainside
Scenic beauty passes by
Brightening up my homeward ride!

Black Eyed Susans in a crowd
Gathered for the 'Bon Voyage'
Happy – huddled – waving proud
Black and sunny-gold collage!

Earthtones in the season's blend
Oranges and subtle browns
The colored tree line never ends
Through countryside and little towns.

A lead-grey sky is all around
The wipers, warned and ready
Rain begins to beat and pound
As back and forth they steady.

The road is slick and misty
It's hard to see the line
Mother Nature's feisty!
And we wish the sun would shine.

Then overhead gets brighter
The highway here is drying
The dark reveals the lighter
And the birds resume their flying.

Some farmlands laid out neatly
In burnt-umbers, browns and tans
A sign – "SOLD OUT," completely
No more produce in the stands.

The harvest time is over
In November – all is done
Except the bright green clover
And the wild deer on the run.

The colors help me unwind
Camouflage and erase
Unclutters up my mind
Through fields and open space.

The ride back home is pensive
With sky and earth in contrast
The journey is extensive
With impressions that will last.

11–01–09

Scents of Autumn

There is a scent in Autumn
That cannot be described
A blend of leaves and chimney smoke
That makes me feel alive!

It stimulates the memory
And takes me back in time
To carefree childhood days when –
Trees and mountains were to climb!

–To playing out of doors
Until the fingers froze
And arguing with my mother
Over wearing Winter clothes!

Counting the days 'til turkey
Then eating 'til you burst
(Observing meatless Friday
The day after — was the worst!)

But once the turkey came and went
The cold was here to stay
Nevertheless — we bundled up
To play and play and play!

I still love the mountains –
From the window in my car
The woodsy earth sensations
Smell good right here where we are!

I hardly fly in dreams these days
– Not lately climbed a tree
Stay Inside when it gets cold
And play less frequently.

But I still embrace in evenings
While through the leaves I track
And marvel how the scent of Fall
Can really take me back!

10–27–08

Thanksgiving Day – May 18, 2003

Welcome home Danny! You're back!!
First Afghanistan — and now from Iraq!

That God would protect you was our belief
Now we pray in Thanksgiving and relief.

Your time over there was a test
You served and you gave us your best.

We prayed hard 'til the days got to zero
When you would return as our hero.

That day has arrived — We thank God!
By His Grace — in agreement we nod.

For He heard as we prayed and we yearned
By His Mercy and Love — you've returned!!

In spirit we join too with those
Who did not return as He chose.

For those families — our prayers will not cease
They're still paying the price for our peace.

His Will Be Done — and not ours
Our Faith will be stronger than Twin Towers.

The future belongs to The Brave
We must not let evil enslave!

On this day — Let us lift up a prayer
For Heroes both here — and still there.

For a country that's broken and torn
That precious Freedom be born.

Our soldiers have experienced the worth
Suffered labor and pain in Freedom's birth.

Danny — don't you shy from our Praise!
You're Our Hero — for the rest of your days!!

Allow us to tell you — out loud –
From our hearts and our souls – We're So Proud!!

May God's Grace shower down from above
While your family surrounds you with Love

May the Love and the Pride that we feel –
Comfort you now – as you Heal.

May your future be filled with success
For your Courage may you always be Blessed.

Let all Good Things come your way –
God has Always been With You – Let Him Stay.

A Heartless Thanksgiving

'Twas early on thanksgiving – and all through the house – family still sleeping – so I was quiet as a mouse

Washed my face and got dressed and crept down the stairs – no bra and no makeup – no worries – who cares!

The apron was hung up by the door on the hook – I fastened and tied it – preparing to cook.

I turned on the radio and went straight to my work – to holiday tunes – I whistled and chirped.

Flew open the fridge door and what did I see – the turkey defrosting – though, not completely!

Then I hauled the big bird from the fridge to the sink – and filled it with water – submerged with a wink!

The legs were bound up with a plastic so tight! – I couldn't unloosen it – try as I might!!

Those legs had to open – to remove the gizzards – so I turned with a jerk – and reached for my scissors!

I wrestled and twisted and called out bad words! – who the hell shoves plastic inside these birds?!!

A wet turkey is slippery and slimy and slick! – I knew in a moment – this was no easy trick!!

I yanked and I pulled and I cut and I snipped! – the
legs finally parted – the cavity unzipped!

My hands how they wiggled – my fingers – so swift! –
at last the liver slid out like a gift!!

But the neck and the gizzard were frozen quite solid –
I hacked and I stabbed with my knife – as I hollered!

The bag finally tore – in which they were encased – I
must have those innards!! – they'll not go to waste!!

I had to use forceps and scissors and a knife! It looked
like a scene from 'Call the Midwife!!'

I poked and I prodded and searched for the heart –
damn if it's missing – that's my favorite part!!

I delivered the gizzards and next came the neck – this
turkey is heartless! – I exclaimed – what the heck!!!

Most of the plastic remained still intact – in spite of
my efforts – and the way that I hacked!!

The plastic was sturdy and white as the snow – whose
ideas was to rig it – guess I'll never know –

Secured and entwined and so deeply embedded – the
thought of my trying to free it – I dreaded!

Whoever invented this – I called him some names! –
preparing this turkey –was no fun and games!!

But into the oven it finally went – my fingers so sore –
and my scissors – all bent!

In spite of the challenge and measures so drastic – the
turkey was delicious! – with no taste of plastic!!

For when it was done and the carving began – the last
piece of plastic I held in my hand.

And they heard me exclaim – as I threw it away –
don't eat the plastic on Thanksgiving Day!!

2021

Surrender!

Autumn bursts upon the scene
I sadly watch the Summer fade
Foliage unfurls its essence
Flaunting colors on parade.

The season graciously resigns
Green transforms to every hue
Phenomenal the presentation
As nature hosts the Grand Debut.

Vibrant Gold and Fiery Orange
Burgundy and Crimson call
Singing out in all their glory –
I find myself embracing Fall.

Misty Multicolored mornings
Coral sunsets – Painted skies
Brisk and Breezy country walks –
Season stay! My glad heart cries.

09–30–06

9. PERSPECTIVES

Buzzwords

Imagine – say 50 years ago
With a genuine crystal ball
Had we but ventured to look inside
Could we have predicted it all?

What would we have thought back then
Of the things that we know now?
Take language – which over time evolves
But who knows when or how?

We humans are very creative
Coming up with catchy phrases
Inventing vocabulary as we go along
With all the latest crazes!

Lots of examples come to mind
But I'll only offer a few –
(This is how I entertain myself
And it might tickle your brains too!)

We like to call them 'buzzwords'
Or 'lingo' with a whole new meaning
(These are the things that I think about
Which explains why I'm never house-cleaning!)

For instance – a bootie – some years ago
Was only a baby's shoe
These days if you 'shake a bootie' –
You're referring to something new!!

For some words are derived from singing
Unconventional songs that we sing
While others are quite versatile –
Such as the well-known 'Bada-Bing!'

Put 2 words together and notice
The message can change with the tide
I thought 'Gangster (W)rap' was some kind of scarf –
Worn in winter by Bonnie and Clyde!!

Oh no! It is totally different
Some actually say that it's 'music!'
(I tried to listen just once –
But my poor mind I thought I would lose it!!)

Who knew that the term 'multi-tasking'
Would validate hard work as an art!
Juggling several jobs at one time??
Why we women did that from the start!!!

Cooking and cleaning and diapers and driving
With or without any pay!
Balancing families and houses and a job –
Throbbing feet at the end of the day!!

Wouldn't you think that a 'melt-down'
Would just be the opposite of 'freeze' –
Or maybe a way to describe
The cooking process of cheese??

Wrong again! – for today's definition
'Melting down' means to have a good cry
Dr. Phil and Oprah use the term all the time
So you'd have to ask them to know why.

I remember my childhood clearly
In the yard with a sibling or playmate
Everywhere kids played with other kids –
Never had to schedule a 'playdate!'

And what's going on in the schools?
There's O.D.D. – O.C.D. – A.D.D.
Didn't letters use to spell words??
(Or maybe it could be just me!)

If my memory serves me right –
50 years ago we only had
One distinction that labeled a kid –
B.A.D. meant the kid was just BAD!!

Now we have all kinds of 'Disorders' –
For misbehaving – one's name can be cleared
'Outrageous' is – just a 'perception'
(No longer such a thing as 'Just Weird!!')

We all ate cheeseburgers back then
But when did we call it 'fast-food?'
America didn't run on Dunkin or Starbucks –
In those days our own coffee we brewed!

'Down-size' is the buzzword in business
But when eating out we 'Super-size!'
(And we even got even with the French for a while –
By referring to 'Liberty Fries!!')

And how about 'Ethnic Profiling' –
Just who's idea was that?
I was always taught to beware when driving –
Of 'an old man wearing a hat!!'

Life was simple – but how things have changed!
There are Terrorists now everywhere!!!
Wrap my head in a towel after I shampoo –
Then go driving??? Why I wouldn't dare!!!!!

Remember we used to eat out
Sometimes with a sister or friend?
Now we no longer just 'grab a sandwich' –
'Let's do lunch' – is the latest trend!

The list seems to go on and on
Buzzwords like 'blogging' and 'texting!'
'Desert Storming' – 'Global Warming' – 'e-bay' and
'feng-shuey' –
Never knowing what will be the next-thing!!

But things haven't changed all that much
We just substitute new for the old –
'Be-bop' is "hip-hop' and 'Groovy' is 'Awesome'
And 'Sinusitis' is still – just a cold!!!!!!!

Recycl–A–Blues

I used to be quite likeable
Before things got recyclable
Now I fuss and sing the blues
While separating my refuse.

What once was used and thrown away
Must now be stashed till pick up day,
I mumble, moan and even shout
Should I forget to set them out!

Don't throw away that soda can!
Into the kitchen garbage can!
You think that's garbage? How absurd!
That's called ALUMINUM – Haven't you heard???

Pizza boxes – here's a test...
Can those go out with all the rest?
Cardboard's garbage – That's for sure.
That's what you think! Not anymore!!

Newspapers – once an easy discard
Are tied and waiting in the yard.
The stacks are getting to be a pain
I hope the truck comes before the rain!

I'm learning how to save and hoard
My bottles, jars, cans, cardboard.
They pile and form a barricade
While through the "empties" I must wade.

Sleeping late – one of Summer's joys –
No such luck – What IS that noise??
It's glass pick-up day! CRASH–BANG–BOOM!
Well at least in the kitchen there'll be more room –

For stacking and storing and sorting more stuff
STOP EATING AND DRINKING! ENOUGH IS
ENOUGH!!
Oh – it isn't so bad – I suppose we'll adjust.
To keep this world turning – I guess we just must.

So rinse out those bottles and place in the pail.
And tie up your wrappings and all your junk mail.
We'll work out a system – there must be a way –
For it looks like recycling is with us to stay.

"F." ed

I try to be guided by Faith
Not misled by my unFounded Fears
But time and again I'm a Failure
As I Fumble and Fall through the years

I'm Filled now with Futile Frustration
For I've Faltered again I'm aFraid
My Foolish reaction to Family Facts
Proved Fruitless – the Fuss that I've made!

What a Fine can of worms I have opened!
What a Freakin' Foul Fish I have Fried!!
For my penance I Forfeit up Family Fun
They'll Forgive me when Finally I've died!!

I Forced everyone to Foreclosure
Of inFo. That shouldn't be mine
Now I'm Forced to Face up to the Fiasco
And stayin' up late with my cryin'.

It's all too Familiar a story
Of a Fallacy Found out too late
Following Feelings of Fearfulness
Functions only to alienate!

I have proved once again I am Fallible
Favor me that you'll understand
From my Flaw to be Fretful and Frantic
The Fires of my Fate I have Fanned!

My Feeble attempts to Facilitate
Flew back in my Face through my Fault!
So Flog me and Feather me – I'm guilty!!
But now – Fury and Fighting must halt!!!

I am Fiercely in love with my Family!
I am Fighting to show that I care!!
I am Finished with asking – what's wrong
If I can Fix it – you know I'll be there!!!

Feverish anger is Fatal!
Stop pointing Fingers of blame
Allowing this Feud to Fester
Is Frankly a Formidable shame!!

Let's Formulate up some Forgiveness
Let's not Forsake one another
Family comes Firstly and Foremost!
Parent – Wife – Sister – or Brother!!!

Love, Mom (Feb. 2004)

Cell Crazy

Are other people sick and tired?
Or am I all alone?
Everywhere I go these days,
Someone's talking on the phone!

Theaters, classrooms, restaurants,
Markets and the Mall,
Even public restrooms –
From within a bathroom stall!!

Emergencies I understand,
But rarely that's the case.
It's just annoying chit-chat
Anytime and any place.

Like – "Hi-ya-How-ya-doin'?
Really? Ha-Ha-Ha-Ha-Ha!"
Trivial conversations,
"Ya-da-ya-da-ya-da-ya."

Ring-a-Ling-a-Ling-a-Ling!
Some make music – some can beep.
Mornings, afternoons and evenings,
I hear cell phones in my sleep!!

Children outdoors with their mommies,
But their mommies do not hear.
Parent/child interaction???
Cell phone's soldered to her ear!!!

Is everyone so self-important
They must always be on call?
"Cell-phone Status" draws attention,
Makes them visible – that's all.

At a Parent/Teacher conference
Came a ringing from her purse –
"Honey – Please defrost the chicken."
Can priorities get much worse??

At a recent graduation
In the middle of a speech,
The "gentleman" beside me
In his pocket he did reach.

"Yeah – What's up?" he loudly whispered,
As he trampled over me!
Someone lock him in a phone booth,
Where he really ought to be!!

Even at a funeral once,
(though it doesn't happen often)
Someone's telephone was ringing,
It was coming from the coffin!!!

Worst are drivers using cell phones!
If you see one – you must stop!
First pull over for your own sake,
Use your cell phone – Call a Cop!!!

Where will cell phones turn up next?
You can simply never tell.
Who'd-a-thunk that they would Rule us?
Go ask Alexander Bell!!!!!

There'll be Peace at last in Heaven,
But what's that Racket down in Hell?
Eternal Buzzing – Beeping – Ringing!!!
Condemnation – by the Cell!!!!!!!!!!!!!!

2004

Garage Sale Tale

Every Saturday morning I scratch-up
A few singles and a bunch of loose change
I've a hobby I call "Garage Saling"
To my family – it's no longer strange.

Over coffee I map my adventure
From the newspaper classified ad
In a three-mile radius I travel
It's the cheapest fun I've ever had!

Look what I got for a quarter!
And this only cost me a dime!!
It really does seem like a steal –
And yet it's not even a crime!!

Household items and good books
I get for a 'song and a dance'
The Sinatra Collection – and candles!
You can't beat the price for romance!!!

What's that? You like my new shoes?
I've a different pair for each day
Why not – when they cost fifty cents?
(A whole dollar – I simply won't pay!!)

That red dress I wore to your wedding
I do hope it brings you both luck
But if not – I won't have to regret it
'Cuz it only cost me – a buck!!!

I get bargains on coats and on sweaters
And I recently got a new suit!
(Not my size – but I just couldn't pass)
If I just lose ten pounds – I'll look cute!!!!

Unique little treasures I bring home
And nick-nacks to put on my sill
A girl can't have too many Crock–Pots
Or a slightly used – George Foreman Grill!!

Funny thing though – My house looks much smaller
I've not as much room as I had
Guess I already know the solution –
I'll just run a "GARAGE SALE!" ad.

'Til I've unloaded some of this clutter
From garage sales I'll have to refrain
With the stuff all re-tagged in the driveway
I just hope that it doesn't rain!!!!!

No more venturing out EVERY WEEKEND
I'm an ADDICT – I had to reform!
No more "Saling" for me EVERY SATURDAY –
Just EVERY-OTHER Saturday morn!!!!!!!!!!!!

07–27–04

Shoe-Shine Man

There's a man who's always been around
Walking through the streets of town
Through the years as he goes by
To see him makes me want to cry.

He is the "Shoe-Shine Man," I'm told
It's hard to say if he's young or old.
As a mark of the years that he has spent
Shining shoes, he's permanently bent.

His humble position serves to remind
That every one of us needs to be kind
Rather than stare – say a prayer instead
That he's able to earn his daily bread.

And there but for God's Holy Grace
Go you or I in the old man's face.
His purpose in life is part of the plan,
Which we are not meant yet to understand.

When his shoe-shining days are finished on earth
The angels will rescue him to show him his worth
God will provide, at the end of the line –
Him with Silver Wings and a Perfect Spine!

Bye-Bye Billy
(Shame on you Pres. Clinton!!)

Hey Bill – Get off of that hill!
Your lies and cigar tricks – are makin' us ill!

You've successfully proved – that you're a louse!
We don't want white-trash in the White House!

We thought you were smart – but Gee Whiz!
How can you not know what means the word "is"!!

How come at the mere mention of "gifts"
You develop a mind that's foggy and drifts??!

And if your job is so filled up with stress –
How'd you find time for the mess on her dress??!

Bad enough that cigars make you wheeze –
But how'd you ever come up with such sleaze??!

(For the man who claims that he never inhaled–
You won't have cigars – when you're locked up and jailed!!)

Secret messages you sent with your tie??
And we always thought you were such a nice guy!!!

Well at least you know you can count on your wife –
(Though Lorena Bobbit did send her a knife!!!)

Jennifer and Paula and Monica and more –
Has prompted this warning from V.P. Al Gore –

314

"Better not find the hand of my Tipper –
Anywhere near the president's zipper!!!"

Hey Bill!! Get off of our Hill!!
Your lies and your phone sex are makin' us ill!!!

We honestly thought you were best for the job –
Before you turned into a Sleaze and a Slob!!!

We've heard you procrastinate and whine –
Now we just want to hear you resign!!!

If you didn't hear is – we could just say it Louder –
BILL CLINTON, EX-PRESIDENT,
GO TAKE A POWDER!! –

1998

Ham I Am!
To the Women's Club after a cancelled poetry reading

I'm glad to be here tonight
I'm thrilled that you asked me back twice!
If your January minutes are right
For the records — I think this makes thrice!!

Carlstadt Women's Club again!
Last year I felt so well received
Last month I re-spackled my face and then
When you cancelled — I hardly believed!
(l might have to charge you for make-up
Fixin' this face is a chore!
It takes 3 or 4 layers to shape-up
Before I can walk out the door!!)

But I understand the predicament
Circumstances beyond your control
You're not to be blamed for the way-it-went
With the punches we all have to roll!

But tonight if someone had called
To tell me at home I should stay
I wouldn't have broke down and bawled
I would have just come anyway!!
(For a minute I was worried but then
I am not that easily shook
Not about to take any chances –
I just took my phone off the hook!!)

But I thought as I put on my face
Lightning can only strike once
Still I've bolted the doors just in case –
Someone tries to pull any stunts!!

I'm just kidding — you know I'm a kidder
It was cold – I was glad to stay home
Truth be told — I was not at all bitter
Why I just turned it into a poem!!

You handled the issue so gently
(The small stuff I try not to sweat)
With the Beautiful Flowers you sent me
You've not seen the last of me yet!!!

I have heard that Fame can be fleeting
Yet I have been called back for this
Indulging me here at your meeting
Is an honor that I wouldn't miss!!

I'm so glad to return to the venue
The unsinkable 'Ham I Am!'
It's good to be back on your menu –
Even as leftover ham!!

02-03-08

Man on a Train

Blue eyes
Crystal eyes
Tinted windows
Clear the vision held within
Clear
And not so clear
And clear enough
And pale and vivid
All at once.

Piercing eyes
Shooting thoughts
Like darts
That pierce and leave
Some strange delicious sting
Calm eyes that wait and soften with your words
Then like the sea transforms
Tranquility to might

And behind
The power and the force
The love his eyes reveal
In a thousand cruel and gentle waves
Magic eyes
Sparkling eyes
Eyes that dance
And speak
And laugh
And cry
And sing
And touch.

Kathie Pell 1967

Nightmare on First Street

End of the week — I'm good and tired —
so fast asleep by ten –
But soon I am awakened
by a pack of angry men! —
Just outside my window
on the sidewalk down below —
Back and forth from 'The Balcony'
shouting loudly as they go!
It's Carnival time on First Street
on Friday and Saturday nights —
With screeching brakes and beeping horns
and flashing car headlights!
Some even blast their radios high
with no consideration —
While trying to park their cars —
disturbing peace in the duration!
One recent Friday after midnight
I was especially alarmed —
By a gang who shouted racial threats —
I hoped they weren't armed!
They were chanting — more like 'rapping' —
slurs against minorities —
Top of their lungs for all to hear —
with fear it made me freeze!
I summoned the police of course
but by the time they came —
They'd disappeared into the night —
it always ends the same.
Not only the guys but even the gals
are equally disturbing!
Partying to and from the club —
after hours is so unnerving!

The nightclub on the corner of First and Broad
is a nightmare to residents there!
It's become an attraction to reckless riff-raff —
and the owners certainly don't care!!
The police will respond if you call them —
but by then the group has moved on.
By the time they arrive the perpetrators have
shattered the peace and gone!
They laugh, shout and curse as loud as they can —
and slam every single car door —
With 15 or 20 minutes of peace in between —
then up the block come some more!
From 10 P.M. until 2:30 A.M.
and often even well after —
The silence of night on First Street—
interrupted by lunacy and laughter!!
A parade of laughing loud mouths —
spill out of The Balcony all night —
On Fridays and Saturdays especially
and sometimes there's even a fight!
Weeknights here on First Street —
Peace and quiet still rules —
But weekends Peace is shattered
by obnoxious drunken fools!!
We expected a family restaurant —
a nice place we really believed! —
Instead, a Vegas night club is here!
We were misled and horribly deceived!!
How did this happen anyway?
Just who is responsible??
How did it ever get approved??
And just who is culpable???
We do have elected officials —
who we trusted to make the right call —

So how did The Balcony slip past them? —
Did somebody drop the ball??
Well none of them are too bothered I guess –
since they don't live near the joint –
I'm sure they are sleeping like babies on weekends
and that is precisely the point!
But just spend a weekend here on First Street
and see for yourself when you're sleeping
How the traffic and drunkenness and noise keeps you
up —
including the horns that keep beeping!!

Perhaps the situation then
would surely be worth reversing —
If just one of them had to endure –
the weekend noises and cursing!!

11–03–15

321

10. GRIEVING

Chrissy

How did we love her? Let us count the ways...

C – was for her Courage
H – for Honesty
R – was for Resilience
I – Integrity
S – was for her Strength
S – was for her Smile
Y – for "YFC" – as she always signed in style!

There is no one quite like Chrissy –
so Brazen and so Bold!
God made her so Unique –
and then He threw away the mold!
She left her mark upon this earth
by the age of 57 –
So God decided it was time
to bring her back to Heaven.
She's up there now with Uncle Frank
and Gram and all our folks –
They're sharing Golden Memories
and catching up on jokes!
Her rays of love are shining down
in those of us still here –
Through Family Love and Laughter
we can keep her spirit near.

Love, Cousin Kathie

Loss

L et us all count our blessings
O ver and over again
S oundly – without
S econd guessing –

– the wisdom of God in the end.

Regrets

Where is the morning?
I left it here for just a little while
To do a simple errand.
I turned for just a moment and
It's gone.
I left it for a task
To help some friend
To speed his day.
And now returning I find
It's late.
The morning sun
Has moved across the sky.
I do not see the world as when I left it.
It's cast with evening shadows and
The night is stealing fast the light.

And what has happened
To the morning?
I left it here for just
One moment
To learn of someone's troubles
To carry someone's load
To a town not far from here.
And I hurried all the while
In hope I'd catch the orange
Before it sank into the earth.
But the sky was only pink stained
Above my destination
And I sigh to think
That time should win my life.

Kathie Pell 1968

The Reunion
(In memory of James Kerwin)

Oh Jimmy - Dear Jimmy
Time cannot erase
The joy you aroused
And your smiling sweet face.

In our frivolous school days
Your happiness dwelt
And now in our sorrow
Your presence is felt.

The last night we saw you
You lifted the fears
Of our joining together
After so many years.

How nervous and careful
We all were that night
That our looks and behavior
Be perfectly right.

So that all those who knew us
Would be truly impressed
At how good we still looked
And how well we were dressed.

Those silly old ways
We thought mattered most
But they melted away
Upon meeting our Host.

It was just what we needed
Before the night worsened
The Happy-Go-Lucky
"Father Kerwin" in person!

He loosened us up
(Turned us all inside out!)
And left in our minds
A curious doubt...

Was he really a Priest?
Did he really go through it??
And "they" said that the Class of '66
Couldn't do it!

I believe we ordained him
At that reunion
And in a way, you might say
He gave us Communion.

We will meet him in Heaven
Someday – and I hope
God lets him surprise us
Dressed up as – The Pope!!

And the "Big Reunion"
No longer holds such a scare
Just knowing for sure
"Father Kerwin" is there.

Oh Jimmy – Dear Jimmy
Time cannot erase
The joy you aroused
And your sweet smiling face. – 1981

Good Night Sweet Gina

(To Mark and Verna Paiotti – in memory of Gina)

Lay your baby down Verna
She'll sleep through the night.
Lay your baby down now,
It will be alright.

Gently take your leave Verna
Softly turn and go.
Gently take your leave now,
Gently, soft and slow.

Her crib is cozy soft Verna
Her blanket's warm and fresh
You have made them so Verna,
You have done your best.

Blow your babe a kiss Verna
Then tightly close the door.
Blow your babe a kiss now,
The others need you more.

Your baby's gone before you Verna
She's Perfect and she's Fine.
Your baby's gone before you,
You showed her how to shine

*

Embrace your Loving Woman Mark,
Enfold her to your chest.
Embrace your Loving Verna
She has shared in Mary's test.

329

Caress your baby's memory
But keep your family's love.
Caress her memory Always,
As she's smiling from above.

Lovely Gina Marie

Who is as precious as Gina Marie
Who was with us for only a while?
Who else has such beauty and talent and grace
Gorgeous eyes, gorgeous hair, gorgeous smile!

Which one of you can fill up your folks
With tenderness, joy and such pride?
Which one of you holds the gift of their love
Like a jewel that she carried inside?

Is there anyone here that can honestly say
That they share the same powers as she?
Show me the power of love in another
As lovely as Gina Marie.

<u>You</u> are as precious as Gina Marie
Who was with us for only a while.
And <u>yours</u> are the talents and <u>your</u> eyes are lovely
And <u>yours</u> is a beautiful smile.

<u>You</u> are the youth who fill up us folks
With tenderness, joy and such pride.
<u>Each</u> <u>one</u> <u>of</u> <u>you</u> holds the gift of our love
Like a jewel that you carry inside.

<u>You</u> share the power of love that is hers
<u>Oh if only you knew and could see!</u>
And I'm sorry that I never told you before
Til we lost lovely Gina Marie.

Oct. 1988

331

Gina's Gift
(On what would have been her Graduation Day)

The weathermen had all predicted rain
The sky all heavy-gray – confirmed their pain.

The people kept their hope, the sky would change
The outdoor ceremony was arranged.

Why can't the sun come out and make this day?
Does imperfection prove to be God's way?

Through gray and heavy hearts, we're made to see
After clouds – the sun shines faithfully.

In spite of all the expert weathermen –
The sun displayed its glory once again!

And while the families gathered on the field –
Pink clouds formed above – her gift revealed.

Her spirit – like the pink and precious glow,
To those who felt her presence here below.

She made certain that their day was blessed with sun
Then softly rained farewell on everyone.

The sunshine that she brought should then uplift
Our hearts – To us she gave her Graduation gift.

06–22–90

Tommy's Mommy

A small boy lay still in his hospital bed
By the side of his bed, stood his mommy.
She smiled as she fluffed up his pillow,
And gave kisses and hugs to her Tommy.

You see – Tommy was terminally ill
And each day he lay slipping away.
But Mommy remained by his bedside for hours,
To cheer him and silently pray.

How fortunate was Tommy to have her,
So faithful to her little boy.
How blessed Tommy's mommy to have him to love –
How he'd filled up her life with such Joy!

They both knew the hour was coming
And the boy asked his mom, "What is death?"
His poor mother stood helpless and speechless,
Swallowed hard and held onto her breath.

"– Be right back son," she said to her Tommy –
In the rest room she broke down in tears.
She prayed for the wisdom and the right words to say
And just wished she could roll back the years.

In the midst of her anguish and prayers,
Came a vision that brought her compose.
She dried up her tears, splashed her face with cold
water
And carefully powdered her nose.

Returning to her sweet Tommy's bedside,
She leaned down and she gave him a kiss.
"Tommy – Death is a little like sleeping,
So I want you to think about this –

Remember when you were just little,
Sometimes you'd fall asleep anywhere –
On the carpet or sofa while watching T.V.
On my lap or in your favorite chair –

Then you'd wake in the morning and wonder
And from under your covers ask 'Who –
Carried me safely up here to my room?'
When really – you already knew.

It was Daddy or Mommy that carried you
To your own little bedroom upstairs,
Where blissful and safely you slept there in comfort,
Surrounded by Love without cares.

– Well, Tommy – I think that's what death is
It's falling asleep where you are.
Being carried by angels to the place you belong,
To your Father in Heaven afar.

There His Love will embrace you forever.
In His house will be comfort and bliss.
Our love's just a sample of Heaven on earth –
Here's a taste of His Love in my kiss.

Hold my hand for the time we're together –
Smile for me as a sign of our love.
Know that the good-byes we say here on earth,
Will be welcomes Of Joy up above!

Now think of your happiest moments,
With your family and friends by your side.
They are but glimpses of the Love of Our Father –
Who will greet you with arms open wide!!"

– Tommy held hands with his mommy,
And fell asleep with a smile on his face.
Both were surrounded by Comfort and Love,
Strength inspired by Heavenly Grace.

We all have the answers inside us.
"And a child shall lead us," they say.
We have but to ask Him for wisdom and strength,
He'll provide what we need with each day.

Let us all come together for Tommy.
And hold hands while we silently pray.
For the wisdom and strength on our journey,
And guidance to show us the way.

For life-everlasting awaits us.
God has proved it through Jesus His Son.
Through Jesus we accept what God sends us,
"Thy will – (but not ours) – will be done."

Tommy's story is here to remind us,
Of the simple truths we once knew –
That God is Our Father and Jesus Has Saved Us –
And Heaven Awaits Us – It's True!!

Love, Kathie Rizzo 02–18–01
(In memory of Tommy Tesoroni
For his mommy)

To Mrs. Teseroni
(In memory of Tommy)

MY SON THE TEACHER

As mothers, we wonder and ponder
Just what will our children become.
We guide and advise them – in schooling and work
And protect them until they are grown.

Then before we are ready to let them –
From the nest they take off and fly!
And we worry and warn them – and pray in our beds
'Til they're home again safely – then sigh.

We dream of their future and envision –
Doctors, Lawyers and Teachers and such
In our prayers we just ask that they're happy and safe
Knowing this can't be asking too much.

Some may grow up and take up their reigns
Some simply will go with the flow.
Others will succeed – way beyond what we dreamed –
It's all in God's plan – this I know.

And who are we to decide what success is
If indeed we believe in His Plan –
It isn't the number of years that we have
That determines the mark of a man.

It's the Impact he makes in the time that he had
That measures his life in the end –
In the roles that are acted as father or mother
Or sister or brother – or Friend.

So whether Doctor's or Lawyers – or Sailors
Policemen, Professors or Preachers –
It takes Someone Special – To Teach all the others
Among those are Parents and Teachers.

Though we learn many things in the classroom
Not everything comes from a book.
This Valuable Lesson came silent and swiftly –
In the life that it suddenly took.

For the Imprint this left on our lives
And For All of the Joy He Could Give –
The lesson we learned this November
We'll remember as long as we live.

So when others speak of their children's success –
Take a deep breath and know in your heart
Your Son Is A Teacher – though he's no longer here –
His Lessons Will Never Depart.

Nov. 2001

Frank From Carlstadt

A man named Frank from Carlstadt
Was a soldier in Iraq.
In church I saw him briefly,
When they had to send him back.

His body lay in state there,
It was all so very sad.
Never knew him when he lived here,
Though now I wish I had.

He truly was a patriot,
A hero through and through.
He willingly responded to
What he was called to do.

Though I didn't really know him,
I know that he was brave.
To preserve beloved liberty –
His precious life he gave.

He made the greatest sacrifice
Any man can ever claim.
My freedom he defended –
Yet I never knew his name.

I will look for him in heaven,
Where every soldier I will thank.
He'll be radiant and smiling –
This Carlstadt man named Frank.

2004

For Bill (In Memory Of)

The world is filled with those who come and go
And each of us is touched by those we know.

Some are drawn to greatness by their deeds
Some respond to ordinary needs.

You cannot tell a person by their car
And credit cards don't tell us who we are.

Those titles which most matter in the end
Are Father – Husband – Grandpa – Neighbor –
Friend.

A ready smile and helpful caring ways
The valid proof of how you spent your days.

Lifestyles of the Rich and Famous fade
Eternity reflects the life you made.

What measure is the value of our worth?
How well we use our precious time on earth.

His message was so simple yet so dear –
To best be what we are – while we are here.

Behold – the greatest epitaph reads still –
The World's a Better Place Because of Bill.

02-10-92

Dear Mrs. Capo

You were there for us always
　Through thick and through thin
Treated us just like family –
　You took us right in.

It gave you such pleasure
　To give and to share
Showing time and again that
　You really did care.

A big-hearted woman
　With such generous ways
You worked hard for your family
　For all of your days.

You cooked like a chef
　And baked like a pro
Loved to travel and shop –
　Always ready to go!

Entertaining was your gift
　How you loved company!
Whether inside or poolside
　With coffee or tea.

Your cakes could win prizes!
　Your sewing – acclaimed!
Gave professional haircuts –
　And your paintings are framed!!

What a <u>beautiful</u> woman
  And mother and wife
Blessed with 3 sweet grandchildren
  Such a <u>wonderful</u> life!

We already miss you
  But we have no regret
For the love we received
  We will <u>never</u> forget

Happy Birthday in Heaven
  With your sisters above
'Til we meet once again
  Here's farewell with our love

Our Jimmy

What a good doggie was Jimmy
Such a warm furry old friend
Fuzzy and soft as a blanket
Loving and true to the end.

Devoted he'd sit by the window
To welcome us home from our day
All ready to cuddle and cozy
And there by our sides he would stay.

Our faithful companion – Our Jimmy
So lovable, perky and pert!
Ever ready to guard and protect us
With his warning bark he'd alert!!

We'll always remember Our Jimmy
He was "Family" and not just a pet
Forever he'll live in our hearts
Our Jimmy – we'll never forget!

That Ron!

That Ron had a way with his words!
He wove them together with wit!
Insightful! – Delightful! – or Absurd!
Just for the sheer <u>fun</u> of it!!

Drawing from his keen perception –
Thoughts and ideas he would whittle!
Assigning a whole new dimension –
Transforming them into a riddle!!

Warm and sincere upon meeting –
A gleam in his eyes as he spoke!
For likely soon after greeting –
He'd tickle your brain with a joke!!

He'd question without even blinking –
He'd pull it right out of the blue!
You'd be stumped and feel your brain shrinking
Surrendering without any clue!

Impishly he'd start to smile –
Precisely his punchline deliver!
Serving up humor in style –
With relish – for he was so clever!!

What will we do without Ron now?
How would <u>he</u> answer that line?
He left without taking a bow –
But confident that we would be fine.

Already the man is so missed –
If we could just hear him again –
He'd probably ask us all this –
"When is a rooster a hen?"

– Or "Why did the nun cross the road?"
– Or "When is a raisin a nut?"
– Or "How did the Hindenburg explode?"
– Or "What kind of knife cannot cut?"

He so loved to make us all laugh!
A quality worthy of mention
Let's celebrate in his behalf –
His levity – relieving our tension!!

Embraced in his circle of love –
A comfort zone without pretenses!
His wittiness rising above –
To challenge our logical senses!!

And so life goes on without Ron –
This riddle he leaves in his place –
"I'm no longer here – but not gone!"
Can't you still see his smiling face?

That Artist – and Comic – and Poet!
Was more than the sum of his parts!
Collectively smile now and show it!
That Ron still lives on in our hearts!!

11–22–09

344

The Story of One 'Miracle-Michael' Rizzo
by Sister In Law Kathie
(based on Eulogy by beloved daughter Irene Simpson)

In a Jersey City tenement,
many years ago –
Lived a young and lovely bride Irene
and her handsome husband Joe
Pregnant with her first-born
she accidently fell –
Went into labor and gave birth
and things did not go well.

The baby appeared still-born –
he was wrapped and set aside –
The doctor was quite certain
that the little fella died.
But Grandma was attentive –
and saw the baby move –
She scooped him up – He gave a cry –
and the outcome did improve!

So little Michael Rizzo
was cherished from the start –
This baby boy – this Miracle –
had won his family's heart!!
He grew to be a handsome man –
and went off to see the world –
In the Army and in Italy –
he met his favorite girl!

They both fell deeply so in love –
and after several dates –
Odette and he were married
and he brought her to the States.
They raised two kids in Jersey
and then to Florida they moved
Through 55 years of marriage –
love and loyalty they proved!

They weren't rich or famous
or glamorous – and yet –
They left a Legacy of Love –
by the example that they set!
A simple man was Michael Rizzo –
He loved his family life –
He's fulfilled his earthly mission now –
reunited with his wife.

Smile when you think of him
and how he got his start –
And keep the lessons and his words
forever in your heart! ...

"Thank God – that Grandma saved me! –
that she saw I was alive!
Or else I never would have
celebrated 85!! –
And never mind this crazy world –
the troubles and the rest! –
Just thank God that you were born –
and always try your best!!"

The one thing I remember most –
about this special guy –
He always said "l love you" –
before he said good-bye.

Rest in Peace dear brother Michael!!! Until we meet
again. We love you! XOXOXOthekath

Remembering Jim

You left through a door in your dreams
And we just want to tell you good-bye.
We miss you already it seems
As we gather together and cry.

We're sorry to be so in pieces
You'd never want us in tears
So we'll try now to speak of the good times
And hold on to those wonderful years.

You were Such a Big Part of this family
You were Always with humor and wit
A light has gone out at our table
In the place where you used to sit.

You inspired us all with your stories
Made us laugh with your great sound effects!
Through the years we have all stayed together
For this we can have no regrets.

The Courage and Strength and Endurance
You showed in your earlier years
Reminds us in times of our own trials
That we too can conquer our fears.

In ways much too many to count
We're so glad for the time that we had
So we'll keep you alive in our hearts
And try not for too long, to be sad.

For we know where you are – you're surrounded
By family and long-ago friends
And we'll join you someday at that table
In the place where our love never ends.

Old Men

Tell me Jesus
The truth is in the rain
Isn't it
Isn't it
Loneliness swells in the rivers
'Til they overflow
And steal a thousand lives
And the people cry "drowned! –
The rain took them all –
The rivers swallowed them all!
Have mercy Jesus!"

But the truth is in the rain
Isn't it
And a thousand of them
Drown each day
Right
And a thousand more are waiting
Waiting in the rain
And their souls are damp
And their skins are cold
And you don't have to touch them
To know
You can know them by their eyes
Red eyes –
Wet eyes
And tongues that talk
Of yesterdays.
And weak smiles that fade
And come again
  and come again
    and pass.

Compassion cannot save them
For they long for the rivers to swallow them
Rain is their hope
There is no tomorrow in the sun
Only Yesterdays
Have mercy Jesus!

Kathie Pell 1968

The Spirit of 'The Twins'

Crisp and Cool September morn'
Change of seasons – round the bend
A cloudless sky – a day so new
A clear horizon without end.

Glorious sun! Pre-Autumn day
The Twins against the sky so blue
With Tuesday morning underway –
Into The Towers – evil flew!

End of Summer had just begun
Children – one week back in school
September 11, 2001 –
Never expected a lesson so cruel!!

Enemies claiming victory
Broken burning mangled heap!
Innocence reduced to ash –
Families crying in their sleep!!

Images forever etched
Smoking silhouette of shame
Searching – weeping – shattered lives!
Angry shouting – 'Who's to blame?!!'

Knowing our guard
Was weakened and lax –
Satan's brigade slipped
Right through the cracks!

Our tightened security –
Enforced way too late!
The death-squad should have
Been stopped at the gate!!

******

Empty space in the skyline
As each day begins –
The Holy Ground Zero –
Holds The Spirit of the Twins.

Like 'The Mighty Phoenix'
Now that we've been burned –
We can rise up from the ashes!
With the lessons we've learned!!

04–29–06

Questions of a Love-Lost

WHEN did you fall out of love girl?
Was it Fall – or Winter – or Spring?
I thought that we had it all girl
I almost bought you a ring!

WHAT time of day did I lose you?
Was it morning – or nighttime – or day?
I can't believe you would choose to
Let me find out in this way!

WHERE were you when you first realized?
Was it your place – or my place – or his?
Playing both was your worst disguise
Knowing now – that it is – what it is!

HOW did you manage deceiving?
I thought you were out with your friends
You really had me believing
That love such as ours never ends!

WHICH one of us is the winner?
Are you happier now than before?
Carrying the guilt of a sinner
I loved you – but you wanted more!

WHY did you think you could do this?
Did you consider the price?
I don't deserve to go through this
Maybe you should have thought twice!

WHO did you think you were fooling?
And WHAT did you really expect?
Love lost – with truth overruling
NOW that you've lost my respect!

WHEN can I ever forgive you?
Maybe in time – but not yet
The shock and the hurt I will live through
– But HOW will I ever forget?

May 2007

Christmas Prayer – 1988

Mary, go look on your doorstep
There's a boy there who'd like to come in.
The world that he left was a lonely place
Decrepit and empty with sin.

He just couldn't see any beauty
The truth of God's love was unknown.
Too many seeds fell among all the rocks
In the places where love should have grown.

You'll know him the minute you see him
He's worried and weary and weak,
It's Jason, the blonde haired and blue eyed boy
With a cute dimple right on each cheek!

It's hard to believe that he left us
Without even telling us why.
Perhaps we did not understand him enough
Although we were willing to try.

There's a boy at your door Mother Mary
Oh let him come in – let him stay.
He came somewhat early – before he was called
Bathe his soul in forgiveness, we pray.

He hadn't the map for his journey
And therefore he just lost his way
Please open your door for this child of God
And take him in this Christmas Day.

To Our Dear Mother, With love
With love to Sandra and Elizabeth and family

Oh our dearest mother! If only we knew –
That your days were so numbered,
right down to a few!
We could have rescheduled, put everything on hold –
If only we knew – if only we were told!

It came without warning, in spite of taking care –
Hospitalized at Christmas! –
so heartless – so unfair!
In the midst of 'Happy Holidays' –
in isolation you stayed
With an empty chair at our table –
we gathered and we prayed.

Soon after the new year – the sad news to learn –
Our lives changed forever – you were never to return.
Our dear beloved mother – if only we had known!
The seeds of pending destiny –
already had been sown!

Oh dear precious mother! –
how could we have foreseen?
This cruel mysterious invader –
would devastate our queen!
Oh darling dearest mother –
if we just had one more day!
All the hugs and sweet affection –
all the things we'd like to say!

357

Instead we're left here holding on –
to our broken hearts –
Reliving your last moments –
going over all the parts.
We know that time is healing –
for you have taught us so –
By your life and your example –
we are strengthened as we go.

We honor you dear mother –
with roses and our tears –
With overflowing memories –
for all the cherished years!
We're grateful for you dear mother! –
for your sacrifice and strife!
Empowered by your spirit now –
we represent your life!

Your legacy continues –
and our love is in your name!
The gifts of faith and love you showed –
forever will remain!
Now rest in peace dear mother –
but remind us now and then –
That our faith and love sustains us –
until we meet again!

2020

With Love from a Shadow

Mental illness – affliction of the mind
Phantom thievery of the darkest kind
That robs a person of their rightful joy
Sad and empty like a child without a toy
I struggle every day to comprehend
And search in vain for answers without end
Depression, Panic and Anxiety –
Paranoia transforming her identity
There doesn't seem to be a rhyme or reason
Sometimes episodes are triggered by the season
At times I'm at wits end – I can't deny
Wrestling with the questions 'how and why'
A 'chemical imbalance' or 'genetic factors' –
'Environmental' or 'relationship reactors'?
For heaven's sake – the 'Experts' can't agree!
So who am I to think that I should see?
Still the love I vowed is Evergreen
"In sickness and in health" is what I mean
Others pity me but no one knows
Among the thorns there lives a precious rose
I'll shadow her until the day I die
For 'There but for the Grace of God go I!'

02-26-16

Love Eternal

I'm just a blink away from my emotions
I'm just a smile away from breaking down
The tears I hold inside could fill an ocean
Beneath this pleasantry – I wear a frown.

Ask me how I'm doing – I'll say 'fine'
To burden you with grief is not my style
But sit with me and share a glass of wine
You'll see behind this Mona Lisa smile.

By day life carries on – or so it seems
With loneliness I never knew before
At night I long to see him in my dreams
Wishing I could hear his voice once more.

In dreams I'm still beside him and we're talking
I see those eyes that won me from the start
Along the shore we're holding hands and walking
Confirming love eternal in my heart.

His memory I recreate at will
I close my eyes and there I see his face
This moment I am comforted – but still
Remains the longing for his warm embrace.

Love suspended in a constant prayer
My ever present alter-ego friend
Depending on his spirit to be there
Eternal soul-mate lover 'til the end.

Solace – only in my prayers I find
In seeking daily guidance from above
One thought keeps on repeating in my mind –
I am enriched forever by his love.

December Thoughts
(Still hangin' on since January)

It's been three long and lonely years –
I think of you Paul. Night and day
I smile whenever a cardinal appears –
so briefly, then just flies away –
Takes with it a piece of my broken heart –
the one you stole from me –
Way back when our love made its start –
and we pledged to eternity.
Still, the legacy of our love endures –
with kids and grandkids we're blessed –
Their happiness and health reassures –
with visits and phone calls when I'm stressed.
I'm sure from your place 'in the sun' –
you can see that the world here has shifted –
At times when I think I am done –
by family and friends I'm uplifted!
I live every day to the fullest –
I learned how to do that from you! –
With joy, I check off my 'to do' list –
which you know is never quite through!!
I'm grateful each day I awake –
'my cup runneth over' so deep!
I am mindful with each step I take –
and pray every night when I sleep.
And I see you in most of my dreams –
like the cardinal – appearing so brief –
You're here and you're not – so it seems –
which in some ways confirms my belief

Or at least that is what I hold onto –
along with the photos and things –
From the fifty years that we've gone through –
some comfort and solace it brings.
Strangely, I miss you and yet –
at the same time I find myself – 'pissed'!
For I'm pretty sure – I would bet –
that by you – I'm not equally missed!!
Though it doesn't make any sense –
I just thought that I'd like to say it!
You know how I am with no pretense! –
I say what I feel – don't delay it!!
Make the lights flicker for me –
or make the draperies move!
Your teasing came so easily –
if you still love me then prove!!
I'm asking too much I am thinking –
so, okay – okay – okay!
But if I see my lights start blinking......
I'll remember how you used to play –
I miss all the fun and the teasing –
I long for the laughs that we shared –
Warming my feet when they're freezing –
stronger our love, wared and tared :)
Alright – I'll admit I am dragging –
sorry to go on and on
My rhymes as you see, now are lagging –
you'll be happy to know – I am done. :)
Sometimes I just have to rhyme –
it's the only way I know how –
There is no one here at the time –
and I'm missing you right here and now!

So. Thanks for letting me vent –
I hope that from heaven you're reading –
I long for the time that we spent! –
your love and affection I'm still needing!!!

XOXOXOXOXOXOthekath

Home For Christmas

I'll be home for Christmas
You can count on me
Peace embrace — God's Holy Grace
Has set my spirit — Free!

Christmas Eve you'll find me
In His Holy Light
Shining Love — in stars above
And candles burning bright!

Memories will comfort
Of the life we shared
Happy noise — and Family joys
Oh how we loved and cared!!

I am Home this Christmas
Death's not what it seems
Love's reborn — on Christmas morn'
I'll see you in your dreams —
Until we meet again.

A Toast to Our Love

A toast to our love on our 50th anniversary!

Another winter's come and gone –
and spring has sprung again.
I'm left behind to carry on –
and do the best I can.
An ever-present ache remains –
a fixture in my heart.
Our happy home with teardrop stains –
each lonely day I start.

Uplifted by the smile you send –
from your photo framed.
Encouraged that my heart will mend –
or at least this longing tamed.
Our 50th is drawing near –
how will I face that day?
I so desire you with me here –
instead I'll go away.

With changes in environment –
the pain dilutes a little.
Retreating like in a tent –
alone here in the middle.
I've so much to be thankful for –
it wouldn't serve me right –
To wallow in my grieving more –
except alone at night.

We shared a great adventure, we! –
a lifelong love affair!!
Put branches on our family tree –
we were such a lucky pair!!!

And life goes on – so I am told –
therefore I shall 'March 4th.'
Together I hoped that we'd grow old –
but alone I carry the torch.
And so I shall in honor of –
our 50 years together –
Come July 4th, I'll toast our love –
and you and I forever!!

Happy 50th in heaven dear Paul!
Wait for me! Love, your Kath

The Sign

In the center of my backyard grows a single daffodil –
Yet yesterday it wasn't there at all!
Do flowers sprout up in the night
and simply grow at will?
And shoot up fully bloomed all straight and tall??

In the center of my heart is an ache that's here to stay
For the man I loved moved on to Heavenly grace.
I cared for him closely by his side
until he passed away
A sign of love that death cannot erase.

Today on Easter Sunday morning –
three days past his leaving –
I look to the sky and heavens through my tears
In search of hope – a sign of love –
to help me through my grieving –
And then – the golden daffodil appears!

Is it just wishful thinking –
or can this flower be a sign?
For me to notice from my windowsill?
The sun reveals its splendor as I witness the Divine –
This tall and handsome yellow daffodil!

Am I being foolish? – Am I captured in the moment?
Just hoping for a miracle to find?
Is it coincidental – or a message that he sent?
Or simply just a daydream in my mind.

Still the daffodil delights me
and I cannot help but smile
Can it be that he has kept his promise?
I stand beside the window – and savor it a while
The possibility – I can't dismiss.

And then I glanced around the yard –
and something caught my sight –
The cherry tree – that never bloomed before –
The cherry tree – that never bloomed –
was bursting now in white!
Two signs from him! I couldn't ask for more!!

Overnight – a flower grew! –
And now blossoms on the tree!!
I knew that he would show me if he could!
He has touched my heart from Heaven –
where his spirit now is free –
He let me know – just like he said he would!

11. WINTER

When I Was a Child

When I was a child:
I asked Mommy what she wanted for Christmas,
And here is what my Mommy said to me.
– Give me your hugs and your kisses.
And drawings to hang on my wall.
Hold my hand when we go to the park.
Let me catch you whenever you fall.

Tell me your dreams and your feelings
Say your prayers by my side in the night.
Bring me your stories and nursery rhymes.
Eat your ice-cream – But save me a bite!

When I was a teen:
I asked my Mom what she wanted for Christmas,
And here's what my Mom said to me.
 – Greet me whenever you see me.
Say good-bye when you walk out the door.
Once in a while, let me hug you.
And show that you love me once more.

Say your prayers, like I taught you, at night.
And tell me your dreams now and then.
Your feelings are very important to me.
How I wish you would share them again.

When I am a grown-up:
Mother, what can I give you this Christmas?
Here is my Mother's reply.
– Give me your smile and your laughter.
Give me your hand if I fall.
Tell me your stories again and again.
See – your pictures still hang on my wall.

Remember me each time you pray.
Share with me some of your dreams.
I still want to know how you're feeling.
– And I still like to taste your ice-cream!!

12–10–90

Sounds of Winter

Scrape – Scrape – Scraping
of the sidewalks 'neath the snow
Shovel – Shovel – Shovel –
Keeping rhythm to and fro.
Friendly weather comments
by the neighbors echo clear
"Another snowfall! – Oh my gosh! –
The 7th one this year!!

Thanks for clearing out my driveway –
I'll help you with your car –
I heard this February's
been the coldest one by far!
Watch out for ice on steps
before you open up your door –
Good thing I bought some rock salt
last week at the store!"

Car doors closing – Tires spinning –
Wheels and engines humming
The fella who lives down the block
just got his snowblower running!
Thumping – Crunching snow boots on
slow and heavy feet
The rumble of the snowplow
as it bullies down the street!

The silent sky above reveals
the airport's closed again –
But in the distance calls
the faithful whistle of a train.

The radiators in my house
warmly hiss away –
And hum a cozy lullaby
throughout the night and day.

The crackling of the fireplace –
The glowing logs unsteady
A noisy kettle on the stove
screams out that tea is ready!
The shrieking of the children's voices
playing in the snow
Awakens childhood memories
of Winters long ago.

Behold the sounds of Winter
as the gift of life prevails
While silently beneath the snow –
The crocus never fails!

Christmas Mourning

On Christmas Eve my mother cries
She needs a sign – Love Never Dies!
Oh Evergreen Tree, to her convey –
My love will ALWAYS with her stay!

Christmas Day brings melancholy
While all around – most folks seem jolly,
Oh Christmas Lights shine EXTRA BRIGHT!
To help her through the winter night.

Let carolers soothe her with their singing –
Let Church Bells comfort, in their Ringing!
RING OUT HEALING – with each toll –
Soothing – Comfort – and Console.

Let friends surround her, warm and cheery –
To lift her when she's sad and weary.
Family steadfast – by her side –
LET LOVE – its arms open WIDE!

And may The Baby in the Manger
Not appear to be a stranger –
May His Birthday STILL be cause
To count our BLESSINGS – as we pause.

'Neath Winter's quiet and peaceful snow
From EVERLASTING LOVE – will grow
To broken-hearts, and those – forlorn
A WINTER ROSE – on Christmas Morn.

12–22–01

The Woods in Winter

What is more peaceful than white covered woods –
against a grey leaden sky
With snow gently falling – Not a single bird calling
In quiet remission am I.

The deeper I travel through Winter seclusion –
the closer to nature I find
My spirit in hiding – My soul still abiding
Entangled emotions unwind.

Sensing the emptiness deep in my soul –
Mother Nature lets down her milk
I am nurtured I know – In the woods in the snow
With tension unfolding like silk.

I drink in the beauty of Winter –
the antidote slows down my pace
Like a lovable child – I am mellow and mild
In pursuit of my dreams yet to chase.

Light as the snowfall my worries and thoughts –
under the blanket subside
The snow purifies – and opens my eyes
Re-assessing the matters inside.

The woods in the Winter in solemn repose –
Silent I pay my respects
All dormant and still – In reverence fulfill
Frozen beauty the season perfects.

Meditation, a shift from the chaos –
An overlapping transition
This layer of snow – buffers me as I go
And lightens my whole disposition!

Gratefulness fills up the emptiness now –
This vision has altered my mood
Is it snow on the tree – or is it just me?
Spilling over with such gratitude!

02–23–10

Winter White

Yesterday was Autumn
The landscape Golden-Brown
Winter came at night
Soft and silent – down.

Nature's presentation
Changing on the stage
An effortless progression
Like the turning of a page.

Branches draped in velvet
Evergreens in snow
Frosting on the mountains
And the valley down below.

So sudden the transition
Am I ready for the change?
The road that lies before me
Though familiar now is strange.

I did not see it coming
The signs all passed me by
Enraptured with the colors
Not noticing the sky.

Here am I in Winter
Bedazzled by the scene
White's my favorite color now
'Til all returns to Green!

Nov. 2007

Winter Watch

The trees are bare
The air is cold
My skin is dry –
I'm feeling old!
       It's Winter.

The days are short
The winds have come
I lost my scarf –
My face is numb!
       From Winter.

My nose is red
I feel a sneeze
Pass the tissues –
If you please!
       All Winter

Light the fire
Boil the pot
Tea and cocoa –
And soup that's hot!
       For Winter.

Bird in the oven
Pie on the rack
Forget the diets –
No lookin' back!
       In Winter.

Families gather
Chestnuts roast
Bottles pop –
Holidays toast!
     To Winter.

Silent it fell
In the night
The man said rain –
But it's all white!
     This Winter.

Gloves on the heater
Boots by the door
No school tomorrow –
Ten inches more!
     Oh Winter.

Summer long gone
Autumn went fast
Springtime will follow –
After the blast!
     Of Winter.

11-14-04

Wondrous Winter Walk

A Winter Walk is a Wondrous thing!
With footprints that follow in snow
Away from Autumn and far from Spring
Frozen in time as I go.

The blanketed stillness of night all around
A silent and soft sensation
That muffles my boots here on the ground
I'm treading on white insulation!

Consistent and steady the rhythm of snow
A hypnotizing distraction
White-washing over all worry and woe
Buffering my every reaction.

A sigh deep inside me releases
Thoughts melt away in retreat
Every problem and care nearly ceases
I can almost hear my heart beat!

My awareness has dwindled to this –
Just walking and watching snow fall
All my surroundings dismiss
Except streetlights that showcase it all!

A phenomenal heavenly rapture!
There's nothing more peaceful I know
No other season can capture –
A mystical walk in the snow.

01–17–09

Inside – Outside – Winter!

Inside my cozy kitchen
I am sipping on some tea
While looking out the window
At the frigid world I see.

Desperate hungry Grackles
Descend and catch my eye
On naked bony branches
Against a blue and perfect sky.

I open up the window
And toss the day old bread
Reward the perching visitors
Waiting to be fed.

Quickly I retreat inside
And shut the window tight
Shivering and smiling
At the crisp and wintry sight.

The kettle starts to whistle
So I brew another cup
The busy birds still feeding
Not a second to look up.

Inside – the radiators
Sing the only song they know
While blackbirds walk their shadows
Out upon the sunlit snow.

02–20–07

383

'Twas The Night Before First Christmas

'Twas the night before First Christmas
And outside the town
Every creature was stirring
'Neath the Star that shone down.

Joseph led Mary
To the stable with care
Knowing the Babe Jesus
Soon would be there.

Shepherds in fields
Who were guarding their sheep
Had just settled down
For the evening to sleep.

When what to their wondering
Eyes should appear –
An angel with news
Bidding them no fear.

A Star shining down
On a stable below
Gave a luster revealing
A Heavenly Glow.

They knelt at the Manger
All night until morn'
For they knew in a moment
The Messiah was born!!

They quick spread the word
Throughout the whole town
The young and the old
All gathered around.

Away in the East
There had been quite a chatter
Three Wisemen discussing
A Spiritual Matter.

The Savior had come!
It was heard they exclaimed
They believe in their hearts
That a new Monarch reigned!

So they traveled afar
And they searched day and night
Guided by Faith
And the Heavenly Light.

'Twas not to a palace
The Magi were led –
The King of all Kings
Chose a stable instead!

At last they arrived
What a Glorious Day!
In exaltation
Their homage to pay!

Presenting their gifts
They bowed down to The Child
Gracious and humble
Mary nodded and smiled.

The journey took years
But their knowledge proved right
For the Christ Child had come –
To us all that Good Night!

Christmas Blessings on us all!

Love, Kathie

The Night Before Christmas – 2014

'Twas the night before Christmas
and all through the house
Something was stirring and I was aroused –
Blinking red lights out my window I spied!
2 ambulances and a cop were parked right outside!!
I sprang from my bed – down the stairs I did fly!
EMT's in my living room! But for who and for why??
Then on the couch with my eyes I did see –
My sweet little grandson looking up at me!
"Oh my! What has happened?" I asked everyone
"He had difficulty breathing – your little grandson."
Even on Christmas eve did they dash
Administered the oxygen mask in a flash!
They treated our boy
with such care and such kindness –
We knew in a minute – these were 'Carlstadt's Finest!'
Then off to the hospital they drove in a hurry –
Reassuring us all – we had nothing to worry.
Our little man Landon returned home around 4 –
We were happy to carry him back in our door!
Our Christmas was saved and Landon is fine –
Thanks to all the professionals right down the line!
Starting with his smart daddy who called 911 –
EMT's and police who came quick on the run!
And we whispered a prayer as they drove out of sight
Merry Christmas to all who came out on that night –
And a new year that's happy and healthy for all –
With heartfelt gratitude from Kathie and Paul! (and
the Rizzo Family)

Day After Christmas 2021
An Epic Poem from me to you – so make a cup of tea first....

Dear friends and family. You know me. Just had to make it rhyme in order to come to terms. Hope you enjoy it despite the length! :) xoxxoxoxoxo

'Twas the day after Christmas 2021 –
When Donna and I went out walking –
The weather was windy but mild with sun –
We briskly kept pace while still talking –
Then without warning I was flat on my face! –
In a puddle of blood on the street!
Crying and trembling and shocked in a daze –
Unaware something binding my feet!

Donna at once called an ambulance –
And stayed by my side 'til it came –
That's when she discovered the circumstance –
That some plastic debris was to blame!
The wind must have blown it right in my path –
It was lightweight so I never knew.
What are the chances? – just do the math! –
To be so entrapped with no clue!!

The flashbacks I'm having give me no thrill!
The crying! The blood and the trauma!
Being lifted off the street like 'road-kill' –
With police cars and sirens for drama!!
I was stripped down and stitched up and hospitalized
And given a bed pan to pee in!!
Due to the covid I soon realized –
There wasn't a room to put me in!!

388

For nearly 3 days I remained in the hall –
Between x-rays and brain scans and such –
Without my cell phone and no one to call –
And no food or beverages could I touch!
An I.V. to prevent dehydration –
And for 3 days I wore the same mask –
This was my Christmas vacation! –
In a gown barely covering my ass!!

(If it doesn't make me lol
then my name isn't Kathie Pell!!)

On the third day I arose from my bed –
After the doctor's diagnosis –
Turns out they found a tumor in my head! –
And sent me home with a serious prognosis!!
First came the good news – not one broken bone! –
And second – no sign of concussion!!
Relieved and smiling I asked to go home –
Then came the brain tumor discussion!

"You must be mistaken! My brain is just fine! –
I'm still working and active and fit! –
That's someone else's brain scan – not mine! –
Go take a second look at it!!"
Quickly a second opinion I sought –
And surgery followed soon after –
Marc gave me 24/7 support –
And my sisters with jokes gave me laughter!!

Flowers, fruit baskets and prayer cards arrived! –
From family, neighbors and friends –
Me, all the more grateful that I had survived! –
Now if only this throbbing head mends!
Next came the chemo and radiation –
30 sessions for 6 weeks – a real test!
Marc faithfully demonstrated his patience –
And made sure I got plenty of rest.

My family and friends kept in close touch –
And I hope that they do understand –
The stress and fatigue are just too much –
With anxiety that I never planned.
For I'm nervous and anxious and shaky –
The telephone makes me all jumpy!
Expressing myself seems so flakey! –
No energy has me frustrated and grumpy!

I'm emotional, tearful and weepy –
People tell me I look fine but I'm not!
I am tired but I don't feel sleepy –
And I find myself cursing a lot!!
Each night I ask God to forgive me –
My patience is sorely depleted –
I'm assured that it's just temporary –
Should improve when my treatment's completed.

With faith I hold onto that thought –
Get up early – get washed and get dressed –
Wear my make-up and the wig that Marc bought –
Exercise and eat well and rest.

I drink plenty of liquids – except wine :(–
Gave up reading books for TV –
Take all my medications on time –
Since the new year – this is the new me!!

I was hoping I might lose and be lean –
But Donna's cuisine won't allow that! –
If the next M.R.I. comes up clean –
I'll be just as glad to remain fat!!
The help that I get is invaluable! –
From Linda, Christine and Diane –
At times I am so incompatible –
I just hope that they do understand.

Marci and Mira have kept me afloat –
With visits and phone calls and laughter!
Even a book about me Mira wrote! –
Now I know I'll live 'happily ever after'!!
Again, Diane and Linda and Christine were great! –
They helped me in so many ways –
'Round my anxiety they managed to skate –
All through these difficult days.

Visits with Luke's family gave me a lift –
And come summer those visits more often
My grandkids to me are a precious gift! –
Their love can make my heart soften.
I also look forward to a showing –
With Paulie and Kristin and family –
How those N.C. grandkids have been growing! –
This time lapse has been way too long for me!

Don't know if I've mentioned him so far –
But on the days I am feeling alright –
My dear friend and 'super-man' Omar –
Takes me walking and holds my hand tight.
My friends are amazing with loyal support –
Their companionship, prayers and good food
Daily made sure that I never came up short –
In spite of my 'roller-coaster' mood!

Though my last M.R.I. showed up good –
And for that I thank God every day!!
By no means am I out of the woods –
For 6 months more on chemo I must stay.
So I gratefully accept your positivity and prayers –
And I hope soon a visit we are makin'
In return I remind you about clean underwears –
In case in an ambulance you are taken! :)

Need a Little Nutcracker

The holidays can really make me tired
So when I feel the need to be inspired
The entertainment section of the news
Reminds me how to chase away the blues.

There's one sure way to soothe my fretful mind
I know somewhere "The Nutcracker" I'll find.
It doesn't matter if it's near or far
I don't mind who the dancers are.

The lights go out – then comes the magic cure
The moment that I hear the overture
The stage become the present tense for me
And all the rest of life is – history.

The fantasy takes hold – and I let go
My spirit freely flies to join the show.
Each second is so precious from the start
Just trying not to blink's the hardest part.

Renewed by dancing dolls that come alive!
Somehow I feel the Winter I'll survive.
The Snow Queen so divine in white ballet
Complete with falling snow perfects her stay.

Her sparkling entourage a splendid vision!
Snow personified in soft precision.
The Sugar Plum Fairy, enchantingly her best!
Coffee, Tea, combined with all the rest –

Transforms me into Clara it would seem
As I am carried deeper in the dream.
Arabian dancers veiled in mystery –
So proud – the Spanish pair entices me.

Performing Russians dancing in mid air!!
Sweet Marzipan release my every care.
The Pas de Deux is still my favorite part –
The drama of that dance still stirs my heart.

The dream subsides – and Clara's sled ascends
The music stops. The magic never ends.
The world goes on again, not quite as fast
The memory of this will last and last.
Tchaikovsky's theme will always bring a tear –
Always another "Nutcracker" next year.

1989

Happy New Year to All!!

It's the middle of January and all through the house
Decorations still hanging — by their tails like a mouse
(hey — it rhymes!)
The stockings in the hamper along with the wash
With my holiday sweatshirts — and sweaters by gosh!
I sent not a card — so it's time for my work
You all sent such lovelies — I feel like a jerk!!
The holidays were fun-filled — I feel so much fatter
Back to Weight Watchers I go — to what's the matter!!
So up on the scale and what should appear?
The 8 lbs. I took off – that took me all year!!

Enough of all that — Let me start the year right
By throwing out cookies without one more bite!
And laying my finger on my computer —
Let me fill you in now about things that are cuter!!
Such as Two Special Blessings that came in the Fall –
Gianna Lynn – third child of Kristin and Paul!
She joined Angelina who's 6 – and Landon – just 1!
(That Kristin and Paul sure know how to have fun!!)
We visited them in their lovely new home
With upstairs and down and a big yard to roam!
They heard us exclaim as we drove of sight
God bless this family with a Love that holds tight!

Blessing #2 is Sofia Lucianna!
To Andrea and Luke – she's become 'Top Banana!!'
They used to think Nino the dog was the 'Tops" –
But that was before they became Mom and Pops!! –
Don't get me wrong – Nino's still quite a cutie –
Staying close by Sofia on 'doggy-guard-duty!'
With Luke as a D.J. – so lively and quick

He knew that Andrea would make a good pick!!
So a wedding was planned and now baby makes 3 –
And Nonna and Nonno are as proud as can be!!
There in the lake house (thanks to big brother Marc)
They work as a family from morning 'til dark.
Andrea nurses Sofia with such gentle care
Luke makes music – substitute teaches – and watches
for bear!!

As for Marci and Elo they're doing Great too!
So in love and still stuck on each other like glue!!
They're happily married and I'll give you 'the scoop' –
They join us in winter for pasta and soup!
They live here in town so we see them a lot —
We join them for barbecues when the summer is hot!
Elo's a tech guy and Marci's a Teacher
(On school nights don't call her — you probably won't
reach her —
She's got piles of paper and lessons to plan
It's best to leave message with her #1 man!)
Elo plays in a Latin rock band – Very Cool
Marci follows on the nights that she doesn't have
school.
She's always been marked by her True Dedication
And the love they both share is a Real Inspiration.

And Marc (as with Luke) you can follow online
Out on tour — making music and doing just fine!
He's blessed to be able to make a nice living
Doing what he loves with the talent he's given.
He's Godfather to little Sofia you know —
And he's risen to the title just like a pro!!!
He flashes her pictures from his little cell phone
– Checks up on her by calling back home!

We follow his 'ventures' on a map on the wall
Always anticipating his very next call.
Thank God he's been safe and he stays quite in touch
We're grateful to God for His Blessings so much!

As for Pop and for Mom — after 41 years
We're glad to be able to keep shifting gears!!
The Best that Life offered we found in our Fam
No Prouder Parents and Grandparents — we am!!
(hey — it rhymes!)
So our holiday delinquency won't seem like a mystery
Paul is now at Bergen Community College teaching
History!
And I too (though both of us did once retire!)
Am teaching Pre-K in Carlstadt — (though my salary
ain't higher!)
Anyway — we are healthy and happy — (at least so we
think!)
And I better start printing this before there's no ink!

With Loads of Love,
Kathie and Paul
Jan. 14, 2011

Author Bio

Kathie Rizzo (née Pell) was born in Jersey City, NJ, the third of seven "military brat" children. Relocating frequently in her youth, she married the love of her life Paul and settled in Carlstadt, NJ where she continues to reside. A prolific poet, she is also a professional elementary school teacher, swimming instructor and belly dancer. She received her teaching degree in 1999 from Felician University. In addition to writing poetry, she has also written and illustrated a collection of humorous short stories which she presents at the Carlstadt Library and for other organizations. In 2006 and again in 2007 she swam across the Hudson River as part of a fundraiser for MS and Leukemia. She is the mother of four children, and has eight grandchildren.

Made in the USA
Middletown, DE
05 November 2023

41999590R00246